DEDICATION

This book is dedicated to my incredible husband, Bobby Randall. Without his love and support, without his incredible dedication to the Lord, this book would not be possible. I am so grateful that he believes in me and allows me the freedom to pursue my God-given vision and talent.

I also want to thank my incredible sons, Ryan Randall and Robby Randall who are supporting me in every way to pursue my purpose and destiny. My daughter-in-love, Katrina, who loves and supports Robby with all of her heart and has taught me so many new things, and comes closer than anyone I know to the "Proverbs 31" woman. And to my 3 Grandchildren, Shalom, Mikha'el and Maryrose—(At the 2nd edition of this book we have another one 'on the way')!! This book is dedicated to leaving a legacy of health for them. Let's continue to walk in miracle territory together and live according to God's plan.

ACKNOWLEDGMENTS

I wish to express my deepest love and appreciation to my Mom, Sue Rogers who has always taught me that I can do anything I wanted to do. I wanted to write this book and I did it. This is my first, real published book and Mom, you encouraged me from the moment I could hold a pen to write a book. We did it!

To my Mamaw who loved me unconditionally. She is looking down from Heaven and is proud of me.

To my business partner and friend, Carol Neal, who has put the spotlight on me this year and because of it God has opened so many doors to the miraculous.

To my pastor, Jentezen Franklin and my church, Free Chapel Worship Center—thank you for speaking the truth into our lives.

To my brother, Buddy—who loves the Lord with all his heart and who is one of my biggest cheerleaders.

To Shan Thomas, who helped me to put this together, get it to print, and miraculously get it ready 'on time'. (More than once!)

To Myraio Mitchell, Sr., who was willing to put "sweat equity" into my vision.

To Becky Harbin, for her love and support and most of all PRAYERS and belief that this book would be impactful! Thank you, Becky.

To all my friends and supporters, to all those who have come to my events, stood at my table, volunteered at my workshops and believed in my dream.

Let's all continue to walk in miracle territory together!

A SPECIAL THANKS TO

Tom Womack Photography—Cover and Back Photos- Thanks Tom for inspiring me to feel confident in front of a camera and for allowing me the freedom to be me!

Matilda's - For allowing us the beautiful backdrop for the cover photo. Located in Alpharetta, Georgia - MatildasCottage.com

TABLE OF CONTENTS

Dedication iii
Acknowledgments iv
Introduction 1
Chapter 1 - Fasting To Reveal God's Direction & Destiny In Your Life 7
Chapter 2 - A Lifestyle of Fasting 21
Chapter 3 - More Fasting Testimonies 42
Chapter 4 - A Lifetime of Fasting— A Testimony to God's Faithfulness— Robby's Story 63
Conclusion 89
Let's Begin—Your Workbook & Fasting Journal 96
What Are You Fasting For? 96
What Are You Grateful For? 104
Fasting Journal 21-Day First Fruits Fast 107
Tracee Randall — Bio 125

INTRODUCTION

This world is in a critical place. Everywhere I turn I see hurting people who feel hopeless. It breaks my heart. Yet, the Bible tells us that we are to have an ***abundant life***, and that God has a big plan for it, and so many of my friends are living paycheck to paycheck in mediocrity. So many people walking beneath their inheritance, beneath their birthright, never tapping into the greatness that God has for them. I see marriages falling apart, people getting on more and more prescription drugs—even small children being diagnosed with depression and put on anti-depressants and anxiety drugs! I believe, no, I KNOW that God has a bigger plan than that for His children, and yet, somehow we can't seem to break out of the cycle that we are living in—we are sick in our minds, our bodies and our spirits. Why is it that we are struggling so much and our prayers aren't being answered?!

In 1997 through a series of events God brought us to a church located about 45 minutes from our Alpharetta, Georgia home. At the time, my husband Bobby and I thought we were Christians. What that really meant is that we believed in God, we believed that Jesus was the son of God, but we had no idea what it was to have a relationship with Him-- to walk in the blessing and favor of God on this side of Heaven. We were "babes", and we soaked up the incredible teaching, and grew, and over the years we matured and began to serve in and lead ministries ourselves.

I will never forget when our Pastor announced that beginning in January our entire church was being called to a 21-Day Fast! I did not understand it, and was not really convinced that this was, in fact, something that God wanted US to do! We believed that fasting was surely reserved for men and women of God who were pastors and evangelists and deacons. But it was not for US-- Bobby who was a local truck driver and I, who was a small business owner--with 2 young boys we were trying to raise. But as our Pastor began to share the scriptures and the Biblical references about fasting, Bobby and I agreed that we needed to experience it for ourselves.

When someone first hears the word «fasting» or «fast» they immediately think that they will have to go completely without food and maybe even without water for a period of time, and when they hear «21-Day Fast» they are totally overwhelmed by the thought of it! I would have to say, that was my first reaction as well. Let me quickly tell you that <u>fasting is *not* about starving yourself or going without food or water</u>-- on the contrary! <u>The purpose of fasting is to strengthen your relationship with God, to seek His direction for your life and to break strongholds!</u> Through fasting, many miracles have occurred in the past and CONTINUE to occur even today! And truly, for my family and myself, fasting has been the FASTest way to God's blessing and favor on our lives!

So many miracles!! So many answered prayers! In the 15+ years that we have fasted (and not just during the 21-

Day corporate fast that our church calls, but in fasting at other times throughout the year) God has always "shown up" in a powerful way! Strongholds are broken and miracles happen when we fast! Fasting is our way as Christians to draw closer to God. There are many books on the subject. Fasting was repeated throughout the Bible-- even Jesus fasted. In fact, FASTING is mentioned 75 times in the Bible, and in Isaiah 58, the prophet shares what happens when we FAST: "Is not this the kind of fasting I have chosen: to loose the chains of injustice and untie the cords of the yoke, to set the oppressed free and break every yoke?" (Isaiah 58:6 NIV) Wow! Fasting sets the oppressed free! Fasting breaks strongholds and yokes off of people's lives. I look around the world we live in and I see people in bondage. They are bound in depression, anger, hurt, unforgiveness. And I am speaking of Christians as well as those who do not know the Lord.

I want to share some thoughts about fasting that I believe will help you! First of all, as I mentioned before, I am not a pastor or preacher. I am not a Bible scholar or even a Sunday School teacher. But my husband and I have been faithfully fasting for over 15 years. We always look forward to the annual corporate fast along with thousands of other believers across the world. This 21-Day fast has been a huge blessing to our family-- to start the year seeking God's direction, to give Him our "first fruits" offering has been impactful and amazing in so many ways! Through fasting we have seen family members delivered of addictions, financial needs met, and many miracles of healing. (If you are interested in joining us for our 21-Day annual First Fruits FAST, contact me via email now! Tracee@TraceeRandall.com)

People who have never fasted or who have never heard of it have no idea of the power it can have! The

Bible clearly instructs the *believer* to fast. Jesus stated in Matthew 6, "*When* you give...*when* you pray and *when* you fast..." It is a part of the Christian life-- or it should be-- just as giving and praying are a part of our Christian walk!

I love the scripture that tells us, «*this* kind comes out only by fasting and praying" and believe me, our family has experienced its own issues that were so horrible, so binding, that Fasting was our only option! If you aren't familiar with the scripture reference, it's Matthew 17:20-21—the disciples had been praying over a boy who was possessed by a demon, and nothing happened—the boy was still suffering when Jesus came along and immediately cast the demon out. The disciples, who had been laying hands on many people and they were being healed, asked Jesus why they hadn't been able to cast the demon out. "And He said to them, 'Because of the littleness of your faith; for truly I say to you, if you have faith the size of a mustard seed, you will say to this mountain, 'Move from here to there,' and it will move; and nothing will be impossible to you. But **this kind** does not go out except by prayer and fasting.'" (Matthew 17:20-21 NIV) This is powerful. There are just some things that only FASTING will change.

I am sure that at times you have felt hopeless in your life. Maybe you felt abandoned by God, overwhelmed by life's circumstances and maybe even a bit angry. Maybe you felt that it was useless to pray, tired, weary, and alone. We have all experienced those feelings at one time or another—these are the times that you should consider FASTing—these are the times that it takes getting serious about it and seeking God for direction and wisdom! <u>When should you FAST? When you NEED a WORD from God over *any* area of your life.</u>

FAST OF 2015

I started this year KNOWING that it had to be different. I knew that I couldn't end this year as last year had ended... there had to be a change—and I *knew* that like never before I had to seek God's plan for my life. Over the last few years that my husband I have been fasting together, God has "shown up" and "shown off" as we like to say. But *this year*, this year has been "over the top." So many miraculous and incredible things have happened since the first 21 days of this year, so much so that in May our family coined the phrase we are walking in "Miracle Territory" and according to God's plan. **Many** of the miracles this year have been in the area of our finances and our business, mainly because that is the area that I focused on during this fast. One of the things I asked God for this year was to give me "creative ideas" and it seems that He has done that—and one of those 'ideas' was to write this book. Those creative ideas have come to me at some of the oddest times, and quite when I least expected it—I have been awakened almost every morning at 4am, and my mind is suddenly flooded with ideas that I have scrambled to write down, for fear of 'losing them' before morning. As soon as I put them on paper I am able to fall back into a deep sleep, and I awake the next morning feeling refreshed and ready to move forward! Another time that ideas have come to me is while taking a long, hot bath. Suddenly the idea will form in my mind while relaxing in the sudsy bubbles! I have taken to putting a towel, paper, & pen next to my tub these days so that I can capture the thoughts immediately! I know that these are the times when my mind is the quietest, when I can listen to His voice without the clutter of the day. Sometimes we must be quiet and listen.

Maybe you are in the same place in your life—as a Christian you know that God has a great plan for you (Jeremiah 29) and yet you are not walking in the greatness that He has designed for your life. Something is holding you back. My prayer is that this book will encourage you and motivate you to experience more of who God is through fasting. What I have found is that quite often even as Christians this is an area of our worship that goes unnoticed, and many churches or pastors never even speak on the subject, nor encourage their congregations to Fast. My prayer is that you will be nudged to Fast and see for yourself the strength and power that you have when you make this sacrifice. Maybe you aren't familiar at all with this concept of fasting and don't understand how it can benefit you in any way, maybe you have never even heard of it until now! If that is you, then "buckle your seatbelt"—you are about to learn some amazing things that can help you in every area of your life!

Psalm 37:4 Take delight in the LORD, and he will give you the desires of your heart. (NIV)

CHAPTER 1

FASTING TO REVEAL GOD'S DIRECTION & DESTINY IN YOUR LIFE

God has put a vision, a dream, a passion in YOUR heart. It is just for you. Jeremiah 29:11, a well-known verse, "I know the plans I have for you, plans to prosper you, and not to harm you, plans to give you hope and a future." He has plans for us, but somehow we never seem to stay quiet long enough to listen to the vision of God for our lives. We live by "our plan" instead of God's plan! Most people, even Christians, never tap into that dream—they are content to live mediocre lives and just "get by" without ever really taking the time to hear from God. When we stop our normal routine and fast, we take the time to listen to the gentle whisper of God for our lives, and His plans are always bigger than we can dream or imagine (Ephesians 3:20 Now to him who is able to do far more abundantly than all that we ask or think, according to the power at work within us).

But, in order to walk in what I call "Miracle Territory" there are some things we must change, some things we must do. We must be set apart from the world and seek God through Fasting and prayer in order to enter into the land of milk and honey!

It was in October of last year that I began to anticipate the corporate fast that our church encourages at the beginning of each year. As I mentioned earlier, I KNEW that this year HAD to be DIFFERENT. There were some areas of my life that needed to be changed, and I KNEW that it would take GOD's favor and blessing on our lives to make the changes that we needed. I believe that it is important that we are transparent and "real" when we share this type of information, and most of my readers who know me understand that "real" is the only way I KNOW how to be, so I am going to be very honest about what we were going through as a family.

For the past 7 years our family had been struggling financially. My husband and I had been very blessed by God to be able to work from home building some pretty substantial businesses, and most importantly for us, we were able to work side-by-side and create our own hours. Don't get me wrong, we WORKED for what we had achieved. We had sown our seeds and "paid our dues" and had good work ethics and good integrity in the marketplace. We had tithed and honored God and put HIM first in our business and in our home, and as a result prior to 2007 we were mightily blessed. We did not take it for granted, nor did we live an extravagant lifestyle. We were very comfortable with our income, but we were able to go on vacations together, eat at nice restaurants, bless many ministries, and live a life that many would envy and call "blessed". But, in 2007 things began to change for our family—the economy shifted, and like many business owners our income dropped dramatically, and as a result we began to use our savings and our retirement to take care of more immediate issues.

Several businesses that we owned began to "dry up" (we were in our desert place, our famine) and finally, in 2013 my husband Bobby was forced back into the workplace. This came as quite a blow to us as an entrepreneurial family. At that time Bobby was 53 years old and took a job on a loading dock, working from 9pm until noon the next day—more often than not, he worked 14 hour shifts of hard labor all night long--while the rest of the world slept. At that time we were celebrating our 29th year together, and it was quite a culture shock for us. It was difficult on many levels.

First of all, the job that Bobby was forced to take was not one for a man his age—most of the co-workers were ½ his age--and it was immediately wearing on his body. Secondly, we had worked side-by-side since 2002, for over 10 years, and this was such a hardship on us! The schedule he worked meant that there would be 3-4 days a week where we would not see each other at all—he would return home after I had left for the day, and would go back to work before I returned in the evening. We were no longer able to sleep in the same bed—he slept during the day in a secluded basement room, free from light and noise, and I slept at night in our bed—alone. In spite of his hard work and overtime hours, we had created some debt that needed to be paid off, and even though we had dramatically changed the way we lived, there never seemed to be enough money to take care of our needs, not to mention our DESIRES. By October of 2014, I had reached a breaking point. I KNEW that God's promises were not being fulfilled in our lives, and I was determined that FASTING and getting serious about it was our only hope of anything changing for us. Besides that, I had tried EVERYTHING I KNEW how to do in the NATURAL, now it was time to give it all to God and seek HIM for direction like never before! (Matthew 6:33 KJV "But seek ye first the kingdom of God, and his righteousness; and all these things shall be added unto you.")

Bobby and I together determined that 2015 would be different. We had fasted as a family for many years prior, had seen some astounding miracles and blessings in our lives as a result. But how many of you know that sometimes we as Christians just "go through the motions" and never really "enter in" to worship and pray as we should. That's where we were. Bobby and I realized that the last few years we had done just that, gone through the motions. We fasted, but never really sought God and *His* direction for our lives in a powerful, meaningful way. The 21-day fast for us, had in fact, become nothing more than a glorified diet and this year HAD to be different!

TYPES OF FASTS

There are many types of Fasts in the Bible. The Bible shares many stories about how and why and when people fasted, and the results that they received through this act of obedience and sacrifice. There is a "full fast" which typically lasts 3 days—this is where we eat nothing and drink only water or maybe some juice or broth for energy. In his book, <u>Fasting</u>, well-known pastor Jentezen Franklin writes, "It was during a forty-day fast that Moses received the Ten Commandments. (Exod. 34:27-28). When Hamen ordered the annihilation and plunder of all Jews, Esther called for all the Jews of her city to join her on a three-day fast from all food and water. As a result, the Jews were spared, Haman's vile plan was exposed, and he was hanged on the very gallows he built! (See Esther 4-7)." There are many types of fasts, but also many different lengths of fasts as well. Jesus fasted for 40 days, Daniel fasted for 21 days, Paul fasted for 3 days on one occasion and 14 days on another. The "Daniel Fast" is considered a partial fast—it usually means that we give up particular foods and drinks for an extended period of time. In our corporate fast, our church typically does a variation between full fasting and the "Daniel Fast"—which means we eat fruits, vegetables, and drink only water.

I am a Wellness & Success Transformation coach. Although my family does eat meat—mostly chicken and fish—we already eat very little processed foods, very little sweets or sugary desserts, and our lifestyle is already one of healthy eating. I knew that for ME, giving up meat and sweets would be very easy. I KNEW the health implications when we eat those types of foods, so giving them up would not be an issue, and certainly not a sacrifice for my flesh. In fact, it would be welcome after the holidays, so this year HAD to be different. Desperate times call for desperate measures. I began to ask God in December what would it mean for me to FAST, what could I "give up" or sacrifice that would be acceptable as a FAST, and how could I tap into the blessing that He has for us and walk in the fullness of His direction and abundance.

After praying and seeking God's direction for me for the fast, I felt that I should do the "Daniel Fast" which meant 21 days of nothing but fruits and vegetables and water—but in addition I would set aside a definite time in the mornings to read the Bible and to pray, and in the evenings as well. Don't misunderstand, I do have a habit of praying, but it had become just that--a "habit" --and true worship in prayer had been set aside in the "busy-ness" of our day. Although we watch very little television, I had gotten into the habit of going to sleep by the sound of mindless TV—and resolved that I would fast ALL television and that I would read devotions and the Bible and pray instead of going to sleep by the TV. I decided that I would spend some time daily being quiet before the Lord, and listening to His still, quiet voice as He revealed His secrets to me about His direction for my life. Let me share for the reader that for ME, sitting quietly and waiting on God is not in my 'nature'. I am the type of person who is 'busy' all of the time—always working, writing, reading, talking on the phone—you know—the normal hectic life that most people have created for themselves. It is very difficult for me to stop my normal activity and 'be still' before the Lord. But I KNEW in order for things to change, I had to make some changes.

As the date for our church's corporate fast approached, I found myself anxious for it to begin. I felt that the "water was troubled" and that it was time for me to do more than I had ever done in the past during this fast. I could not wait for the fast to begin. I began to journal about this fast. Here are a couple of excerpts from my journal as I prepared to seek the Lord through fasting and prayer:

12/27/14 "I am so excited about starting our corporate fast that begins on Sunday. 2015, the Year of Increase! My prayer is, "Lord, show me the path that you have selected for me—I want to be closer than ever before to You during this fast. Make me bold for You, Lord! Give me strength to keep my fasting commitment so that these 21 days will be as Daniel fasted—I will hear Your voice and Your purpose for my life! I want Your direction, not mine! May 2015 be the year that EVERYTHING changes and without fail we put You first and listen and hear Your voice! A year of miracles! The enemy does not like it when we fast. 'First Fruits Fasting'! I am fired up for it!"

(Little did I know that this entry in my journal would come to pass in such a dramatic and powerful way. A year of miracles!!)

Another journal entry:

12/28/14 "*Many people have been asking me about how, why, when we fast—and I thought it would be awesome to share more about it here—this year, 2015—there is so much anticipation and there is a rumbling in my spirit that tells me something AMAZING is about to happen. God is going to reveal some NEW THINGS to me this year, and it will begin with my first fruits of FASTING! This fast will be at least our 15th year of first fruits fasting, and I don't have time enough or paper enough to share with you all that God has blessed us with through fasting. Admittedly, some fasts have been more powerful than others. But THIS YEAR! This year everything will change because I am READY for change. I am READY to be challenged and uncomfortable! The 2015 fast for our church begins on Sunday, Jan 4th. Counting 21 days it will end on January 24th. First fruits! Pastor is calling it 'The Year of Increase!' I believe it. I receive it! I am ready!*"

1/4/15 "*First Day 21-Day Fast. What a powerful WORD today at church on Fasting! I thank God for my pastor-- 'when you Fast, when you pray, when you give' the Bible says in Matthew 6. I am EXPECTING great miracles. Fasting releases miracles! ((Fasting here is not the same as a food fast-- a food fast cleanses the body, a spiritual Fast cleanses the soul)). I love love love this scripture- Ezra 8:21- 'I proclaimed a Fast there beside the Ahava Canal, a Fast to humble ourselves before our God and pray for wise guidance for our journey—all our little ones and possessions.' Little ones are our children (no matter how old they are and our grandchildren). Fasting breaks generational curses off of families. I am soooo ready & prepared for this Fast like never before. I have been in a dry place but the anointing is coming on me, the oil is flowing & I hear the sound of ABUNDANCE! Abundance in all things! Health, relationships, love, business, giving! 21 Days dedicated to seeking God to reveal my purpose in life! To reveal hidden things. Powerful! Pastor talked about the food we eat & how it is the same as the kings who were worshipping false gods-- as Christians we should not be a part of the crowd, we should STAND OUT in health ((we would if we were eating right!)). Confirmation that He has already ordered my steps in teaching people how to eat as God intended, even in the world we live in! I am so ready!*

#Fast2015 #2015YearOfIncrease #HealthyEatingCleanTemple"

Immediately as we began the Fast of 2015, I had a peaceful anticipation that God was about to "show up" in a powerful way. In looking back at these journal entries that were written a few days prior to and the day that the fast began, it is overwhelming to look back at all that God has done THIS YEAR and see that my written words were prophetic in so many ways.

I will give you some specifics because it is so important that the reader understands the POWER of fasting, and how miracles can be released in every area of our lives when we fast! Personally, I was in a very dry place, but as I began to PRAY, FAST and seek God, He began to ignite the hidden desires of my heart!

I have always had a passion for wellness, and had *claimed* to be a wellness coach for many years, but in January of 2015 I certainly was not "known" or recognized as a wellness coach, nor did I have any clients! Another desire of my heart is to speak publically—I have always enjoyed speaking in front of a group, but again, I had never been asked to speak anywhere or to anyone before this Fast began. I headed up several networking groups in my community, but I certainly was not a "paid speaker". As I began to pray and JOURNAL, my love for writing was awakened, and my desire to have a published work began to spring forth within my spirit. I truly didn't have a clue as to how any of these desires would come into fruition, but I decided to *trust God* and write them down expressing that I wanted to build a business utilizing all 3 of these talents and passions: 1) Wellness coaching 2) Public Speaking 3) Writing. *Plays, Movies, Directing, Preaching, Conferences/Workshops*

One thing that I have learned is that DURING a fast it is very typical that nothing much happens in the way of answered prayer or "miracles". In fact, it is sometimes DURING a fast that the enemy begins his attack, trying to take the focus off of what is important and distracting us from our commitment to seek God with all our might. This year was no exception. However, I believed that if I would continue to seek Him this year would be different, so I did not allow the attacks of the enemy to stop me from seeking God and His will for my life. I prayed and read my Bible. I listened to sermons and teachings by our pastor and other men and women of God who I knew were visionaries and would inspire me to stay committed. God began waking me up (as I mentioned earlier in this book) with incredible ideas that I had never thought before. I wrote them down and excitedly shared them with my husband and sons and claimed God's victory over our finances as if it had already happened.

THE ENEMY WILL TRY TO STOP YOU

In February the enemy hit me so hard with a blow that normally would have knocked the vision and energy right out of me. Someone I trusted in business completely let me down, and what I thought was going to be a huge door opened, closed with such force that it took me to my knees and almost knocked the wind out of me. (John 10:10 (NIV) "The thief comes only to steal and kill and destroy...")

The Fast had been over for 2 weeks, and the ideas that God had given me seemed to be stopped suddenly and without warning. This caused me to walk stronger in the faith that He was directing my path, but with finances truly wavering and my sweet husband working 50-60 hours per week all night long, I considered finding a part-time job to help us get through the rough places financially. I began asking God what job would it be? Where would I work that would allow me some freedom to pursue my true destiny, but the money we needed to dig ourselves out of the hole we had dug and to allow my husband, Bobby, some relief from the long hours he was working to support our family? I applied for a job at a local weight loss clinic, deciding that working in a place where I could utilize my gifts would be a good place to start. I was called immediately for an interview, and met with the supervisor to find out more. It was an awesome opportunity! It was just a few moments from our home, I LIKED the women I would be working with, I endorsed their program as one that was healthy....but the problem was I would be working 5 days per week, 8am-7pm which meant absolutely no free time to pursue the dreams and vision that God had given me DURING the fast. The pay was fantastic. I was torn because of my guilt for what Bobby was doing and my desire and passion for what I was believing God was about to do!

    I told Bobby about the opportunity and watched him as he listened intently. What an incredible man of God I am married to! He said to me, "Tracee, we both know that if you take this job it would help us right now financially, and take a little pressure off of us. But more than anything else I want YOU to hear from God about this. I want you to walk in the destiny that God has for you, and I don't think this is it." Wow. I called the woman back the next day and told her exactly why I couldn't take the job. She answered back, "You have an incredible husband. We would love to have you, and if, even a year from now you decide this is what you want to do, call me. I appreciate your honesty. I hope that you find everything that God has for you." Tears of joy were rolling down my cheeks as I thanked God for His direction and for the discernment of Bobby to hear from God and support me in my vision. SOMETIMES WE MUST RECOGNIZE A DOOR THAT IS SHUT IS JUST AS IMPORTANT AS A DOOR THAT IS OPENED! (Revelation 3:7 NIV "These are the words of Him who is holy and true, who holds the key of David. What He opens no one can shut, and what He shuts no one can open.")

THE ENEMY WILL TRY TO STOP YOU, BUT GOD!

When God shuts a door He is faithful to open another! God is ALWAYS working things out for our good—even when we do not see it! (Romans 8:28) 3 days later my phone rang. It was a woman I had met many months previously at a networking event. She told me that she had read a story I had written on Facebook back in October, and I had alluded to dealing with self-esteem and self-hate issues as a teenager growing up. Her WOMEN'S MAGAZINE was looking for fresh new writers who had a story to tell, and she wanted to know if I would write a short article on my story for her March edition. My mouth began to tremble with excitement and the goose bumps that I feel when "it's GOD" rose up on my arms. "Absolutely" was my answer and I hung up the phone screaming in excitement as my desire to be a "published writer" was about to come to fruition!

I wrote the story, submitted it—felt like a million bucks—and continued to claim victory! The article was released in March, and although there was no monetary gain, my self-confidence and vision grew bigger!

March 17, 2015. My phone rang. It was another woman I had met in late 2014 who was a radio talk show host. I had told her of my work in helping families nutritionally with cancer, and she had remembered me and wanted to know if I would be a guest on her radio show! "Of course," I smiled, "but would you mind if I spoke about my self-esteem and self-hate issues instead?" I asked. "I just wrote an article for a women's magazine about it, and would love to promote that article on your show." She loved it! "Of course!" Then she said something else. "You know, I just interviewed an incredible man a couple of weeks ago on my show. His name is Jim Britt and he is putting together a book collaboration and is looking for writers who have changed and have a story to tell—he is a best-selling author, motivational speaker, and incredible. I'll give you his email address and let him know I sent you. I think your story would be powerful in his book." Again....my heart jumped, my mind began to swirl as I saw the hand of God working so dramatically and powerfully in my life!

GOD WILL BRING THE RIGHT PEOPLE INTO YOUR LIFE

IN ORDER FOR GOD TO FULFILL HIS VISION FOR YOUR LIFE, HE WILL BRING THE RIGHT PEOPLE INTO YOUR LIFE AND TAKE THE WRONG PEOPLE OUT.

April, 2015. I received an email response from Jim Britt asking if we could speak the following Monday about the book collaboration, "The Change". During the conversation I learned that he is one of the most powerful motivational speakers alive today, has multiple best- selling books and intended for "The Change" to be another best-seller. I was to write a chapter in book 6!! I asked him during our phone call how he knew I could write?! He laughed and told me he had "googled" me and read my blogs! (I had started a blog in January *during* the fast as a result of a prompting from God to do just that!) He was so complimentary towards me, so humble for a man who is acclaimed by the world AND a self-made multi-millionaire!

The rest of the story that has happened to me and for me this year is nothing less than miracle after miracle after miracle! God has opened so many more doors for me that I truly cannot begin to share them all—since April I have been catapulted into the public eye and have been asked to speak at multiple events and seminars. I have several new business partners and new business ventures that have been PROFITABLE and promise to create an income that will allow Bobby to retire and pay off the debt that the last couple of years of famine have caused us!

As of the date of this writing, I have 3 more books that will be published within the next couple of weeks, and THIS ONE which I am so excited about because it gives glory to God for all His blessings and for the abundance in our lives. I am very excited about my own book collaboration titled, "The Voice That Changed Everything—A Book of Gratitude". In it I am opening the door for others to be published and to give thanks to the person in their lives who spoke greatness into them! It was during one of my workshops titled "Make Up Your Mind" that I coined the phrase #MiracleTerritory. We are indeed living in #MiracleTerritory and according to #GodsPlan! It all started with a commitment to fast, to seek God, and to put Him first in EVERYTHING that we do!

God has given you a dream, a passion, a burning desire that will make you feel alive when it is fulfilled. Fasting will help you tap into that vision that He has for you. He will give you ideas, creative thoughts that only He knows, and if you are quiet and hear His voice, He will give you those desires! I encourage business owners to join us at the beginning of each year to set some time aside to fast, seek God and be a part of our 21-day corporate fast! God will honor our sacrifice, it pleases Him. In this world in which we live I cannot imagine trying to build anything unless God's favor, blessing and POWER is on it! (To learn more about joining us in our annual 21-Day corporate FAST, email me at Tracee@TraceeRandall.com)

I also encourage you to consider Fasting throughout the year—a one day, 3-day or 7-day fast are all great ways to draw closer to God. His word says, "But seek first his kingdom and his righteousness, and all these things will be given to you as well." (Matthew 6:33 New International Version)

This year God has opened more doors than ever before, but He has shut some as well. I have accepted those shut doors and thanked Him for them! I told Him that whatever door He opened I would walk through, and just as I prophesied in my journal, I have been stretched and challenged and changed!

Matthew 6:33 (KJV) But seek ye first the kingdom of God, and his righteousness; and all these things shall be added unto you.

CHAPTER 2

A LIFESTYLE OF FASTING

As you begin to FAST and experience the awesome power of FASTING, as God begins to reveal more to you, you will realize that we have missed out on so much that God has to offer us! As I mentioned, my husband and I have been involved with a church that fasts together corporately each year, typically starting it on the 1st Sunday of the year and for 21 days thereafter. Each person is encouraged to choose their own fast—with the "Daniel Fast" typically being the most popular for a fast of 21 days. There are many ways to fast, but for the purpose of this book and this chapter, I am going to focus on the "Daniel Fast" and also share with the reader what God **REVEALED** to me while fasting this year. Let's discuss first what the "Daniel Fast" is, what is typically meant by "Daniel Fast" and why it is popular as a fast. The "Daniel Fast" comes from the book of Daniel, and refers to the foods that Daniel ate on a regular basis.

When Daniel and several other Hebrew boys were taken captive and brought to Babylon to educate them and give them military training, they were immediately given the "royal food" or "King's meat" to eat on a daily basis. These meals included foods that were forbidden by God to eat, so Daniel asked if he could eat *only* those foods that *HIS* God had commanded him eat. The chief official was concerned that Daniel would become weak or even sick if he did not eat from the King's table, but Daniel insisted and asked him to agree to a "test"—that was, to allow him and a few others to eat according to God's plan for just 10 days. At the end of the 10 days they would re-evaluate, and if Daniel or the others were not as healthy as they should be, Daniel agreed that he would eat whatever was put before him. After 10 days of eating as God had instructed him to eat, he and the other boys were found to be *the brightest, strongest, most mentally alert, and healthiest of any in the kingdom* and therefore they were allowed to continue to live this lifestyle for the *3 years* of captivity. (This is found in Daniel 1)

The foods that Daniel's diet consisted of were mostly vegetables, fruits, whole grains, nuts (seed based foods) and water. He drank no wine or ate no meat. One of the reasons that our modern Christian world has adopted the "Daniel Fast" is because most of us eat from the "royal table" on a regular basis. Our daily lives consist of eating meats, breads, "sweets", drinks with caffeine, processed foods, and foods that are unhealthy to our bodies. We eat junk like chips and dips and lots of coffee and sodas. We eat foods covered and smothered in gravies and cheeses. It is difficult for us to "lay down" the desires of our flesh, and that is where fasting comes into play. Fasting is 'giving up' or sacrificing our flesh in order to become closer to God. Fasting is pulling away from the normality of life and creating an empty space for God to fill!

In our modern-day fasting when we refer to the "Daniel Fast", we typically stop eating meats, sugars, processed foods, sweets, breads and drinks other than water. What is left would be vegetables, fruits, and nuts. The "Daniel Fast" is typically done for 21 days and many churches will call a corporate 21-day fast at the beginning of each year.

But why is it, that typically when we refer to the "Daniel Fast" it is 21-days? Nowhere in chapter 1 of Daniel is the reference made that Daniel ate this way for just 21 days—in fact, the test was done in 10 days and then after the king agreed that this was in fact HEALTHY and he allowed Daniel to continue with this lifestyle for the next 3 years.

It was this question, "why 21 days?" that began to burden me this year (for the first time) while fasting. As I was reading the Bible during the 21-day fast, I naturally began reading in the book of Daniel, trying to understand the power and significance of fasting. As we have often heard as Christians, we can read the Bible one day and our understanding is one way, and then the next time we read it we can have a new revelation about it, a new understanding and God can show us something that we have never seen before! That's what happened for me as I began to read the story of Daniel.

Take a look at this commentary regarding Daniel 1 and Daniel's refusal to eat from the King's table:

"The narrative of the Biblical story is set in Babylon, where Daniel, three friends, and fellow captives have been brought for education and military training. The king honors them by offering luxurious royal foods, hoping to encourage their development. Though young, Daniel had already seen the harmful effects of meat, wine, and other decadent foods on physical and mental health. Daniel refuses to eat foods forbidden by God, and instead asks for "pulses". The guard charged with their care expresses concern for their health, so Daniel requests a short test of the diet. For 10 days, they are permitted to *eat just plant foods.* At the end of just 10 days, the guard is surprised at their good personal appearance and physical and mental health, compared to those who had indulged in the royal foods. Therefore, Daniel and his friends are permitted to eat whole plant foods for the *duration* of their training. After continuing with the diet during three years of training, they are judged by the king to be mentally superior."

Suddenly God revealed to me that this "Daniel Fast" that we called it was, in fact, a LIFESTYLE of HEALTHY EATING, which was why Daniel and the rest of the boys had the best health in the kingdom and were, in fact, "mentally superior"!

As a Wellness & Success Transformation Coach most of my clients are dealing with 2 very powerful and serious issues—sickness and lack of finances. I have watched too many children die with disease, families broken apart due to lack of money, lives torn apart because of both of these issues. During this year's 21-Day Corporate Fast the Lord revealed to me clearly that as *Christians* we are to live a *lifestyle* of fasting. We are living in a time when Christians must take a stand, we must be set apart--yet Christians are as sick (in some cases sicker) than the people of the world! This is a true tragedy! In fact, it breaks God's heart. He sent His Son to die on the cross, but also to take the stripes on His back in exchange for our healing! We are *called* to Fast, to set aside times throughout the year to sanctify and to seek God's direction through Fasting, but we also honor God when we live a lifestyle that is holy and pure!

As Christians not only are we to be set apart in what we watch, what we read, the music that we listen to, the words that we speak, we are also to be set apart in the food we eat. Just as Daniel refused the King's meat, so must we as Christians refuse the foods that are the root of disease and bad health. The church must change first. The Bible says that Daniel proved to the King that his *lifestyle* was healthier and as a result Daniel was "fair in skin" and strong and sharp mentally. It is simple—God designed our bodies to run on healthy food!

The church is as sick as the world. In order to change this, we must be willing to change. Our family made that change 8 years ago and now mostly eat the same food that Daniel did. During this Fast God revealed to me that it should be the "Daniel Lifestyle"! Impossible? No! Nothing is impossible with God!

So why then, is it common practice to do a "Daniel Fast" for 21 days? The answer lies in Daniel, chapter 9. Here's what happened—Daniel knew that the time had come that he must pray for mercy on Jerusalem, even though they had been disobedient to God and did not deserve His mercy. Daniel 9:2-3 " In the first year of his reign, I, Daniel, understood from the Scriptures, according to the word of the Lord given to Jeremiah the prophet, that the desolation of Jerusalem would last seventy years. ³ So I turned to the Lord God and pleaded with him in prayer and petition, in *fasting,* and in sackcloth and ashes." So Daniel made the decision to FAST before the Lord.

Sackcloth and ashes were also used as a public sign of repentance and humility before God. They were used during a time of mourning, showing reverence to God. Just as others had done before him, during a time of great trial and tribulation, to seek God's attention and favor, Daniel *fasted.*

Here's what God revealed to me here--the foods that he ate were his LIFESTYLE and clearly listed in chapter 1. So, again, why 21 days? Here's what the Bible says, "Then he said to me (in this reference "he" is the angel that appeared to Daniel as he was praying), 'Do not be afraid, Daniel, for from the first day that you set your heart on understanding this and on humbling yourself before your God, your words were heard, and I have come in response to your words.[13]" But the prince of the kingdom of Persia was withstanding me for twenty-one days; then behold, Michael, one of the chief princes, came to help me, for I had been left there with the kings of Persia...." So—it took 21 days for the angel to finally get to Daniel--the enemy had tried to stop him (the prince of the kingdom of Persia), but he made it through—it just took 21 days! Daniel 10:3 "I ate no delicacies, no meat or wine entered my mouth, nor did I anoint myself at all, for the full three weeks." I have heard many times pastors preach that when we fast and pray and humble ourselves before the Lord for 21 days as Daniel did, we can expect breakthroughs in our lives!

As I read through Daniel during this year's fast, God distinctly revealed to me that I am to share this revelation. In order for Christians to be healthy we should adopt Daniel's lifestyle as our own—that is, begin to honor our bodies as temples of the living God and quit eating junk and foods that are causing disease and sickness! It's a tough message. Even Christians do not want to face the facts—that the food that we eat today is slowly killing us—and what is surprising is that those same foods were also causing issues with people back in the day of Daniel as well—it is evidenced in the fact that Daniel and those who were eating according to God's law were the healthiest and the most intelligent in the entire kingdom! Most Christians today would argue that we are no longer under the law, and the food laws were abolished when Christ came and died and rose again—his GRACE took the place of the law. That is true, what we eat is not a Heaven or hell issue, but it IS true that God designed our bodies to be fueled with a certain type of food, and we are killing ourselves daily as we eat the processed foods that we know are unhealthy!

As soon as I had this revelation, that we are to eat exactly as Daniel ate as a LIFESTYLE, not just a fast, I began to ask God why He revealed this to ME and HOW He expected me to convince millions of Christians to change what they are eating?! Why me, Lord? His answer was simple and humbling. He said to me, "You asked me what it was that I would have you to do. I gave you this passion to help people heal for a reason, and I trust you to share this message to my people." He told me, "My people must be healthy during this time. We need them to be strong and lead those who do not know me. The world is only getting darker and darker, so my people must remain healthy and strong for the work that is set before them." I heard His voice clearly in my spirit. I argued this point with Him. "Lord," I said. "What if they laugh at me and will not listen?" I could almost see Him smile at my lack of faith, in spite of the miracles that were happening all around me! "Leave the hard part up to me." He promised. "You just share what I am showing you, and I will open the doors to the right people at the right time. My people cannot continue to go to the altar Sunday after Sunday praying for healing and expect the world to follow them. They must be set apart from the rest of the world."

I took a deep breath and decided that I would wait on the Lord to see how He wanted me to share the revelation and the message that He had given me. One morning, I was sleeping very deeply when suddenly my eyes popped open and I heard His voice say these words, "It's time for you to write a book on fasting. The title will be <u>The FASTest Way</u>

to God's Favor and Blessing and in it you will share testimonies that will raise the faith of those who read it AND you will share the revelation that the "Daniel Fast" is not a Fast at all, but rather a lifestyle that I am calling my people to during these end times." I quickly wrote down the title of the book and the next morning I began texting several strong Christians that I knew who had Fasted in the past to share their testimonies of God's faithfulness during fasting.

EAT ACCORDING TO GOD'S PLAN

I began to speak more boldly about eating according to God's plan—about living a lifestyle that was similar to the way Daniel ate on a regular basis, and I began to take it more seriously for myself and my own family.

My daughter-in-Love, Katrina has been receiving the same revelation from God in regard to what she was feeding her children, my grandchildren. She repented for feeding them foods that were not as healthy as they should be, and began teaching them the importance of eating "God-Made Food." She had slowly been making this same lifestyle transition and the benefits were amazing and no sickness in our family! This includes my husband, 2 sons, a daughter-in-law and 3 grandchildren, ages 4, 2 and 1 year old! Today, at 55-years-old, I look younger and feel younger than other women my age, I am healthier than ever before, I have not had so much as a headache since 2007, and have more energy than *all* the women I know!

I share this because God showed me that by making some very simple changes in what my family eats and drinks daily, He has blessed us with extremely good health—even as others around us are sick and getting sicker—there is not a sick one among us! Just as the Israelites were traveling through the desert in search of the promised land, God FED them with manna from heaven, and as long as they ate the food He supplied them, there was not a sick one among them (Psalm 105:37)! Miraculous, yes! Well, according to the Bible, God is the same today, yesterday and forever (Hebrews 13:8)! Therefore, He has supplied us today with "manna"—that is, food that is healthy for us if only we would eat according to His design! The trouble is, we are easily bored with healthy food, and our flesh craves foods which are in fact unhealthy. We eat, drink and live a lifestyle of high stress and such confusion that it is no wonder we are sick and dying!

I truly still wonder how it will be that God uses this simple book on Fasting to change the health of the world. I also wonder how He parted the Red Sea and caused Jonah to be swallowed by a whale. I am sure that Moses was completely baffled as to why he was chosen to lead an entire nation out of bondage. He certainly didn't have the qualifications that it would take to do such an amazing feat. In fact, he too argued with God and asked Him to choose someone else. I am not trying to compare myself to Moses, but what I do know is that if Christians are going to change what they eat and adopt a lifestyle of eating like Daniel ate, it WILL take a miracle from God. So I am just trying to be obedient.

There will be those who read this and wish they hadn't! They will feel a tugging of the Holy Spirit saying, "It's you I am speaking to." And they will do their best to turn their back on this information and believe it is just too hard. But we serve an amazing powerful God. We say, "I can do all things through Christ who strengthens me," but sometimes we are just quoting scripture, not living in the fullness that God has for us! I am guilty as charged. But this year I made up my mind that I would do anything and everything God called me to do, no matter how difficult or confusing that may be. This is one of those things.

Our God, the same yesterday, today and forever! Our God, who sometimes did things just to see if someone would be obedient, just to test their faith. I am reminded of Naaman who was told to dip into the Jordan River 7 times, no more, no less, and he would be healed of Leprosy. Even though he didn't understand WHY God commanded him to do that, he did it anyway, and yes, he was healed instantly. (2 Kings 5:1-19) And then Jesus, who by saying the *Word* could have healed the blind man, instead reached down and picked up mud which he then put on the blind man's eyes, and they were miraculously opened. (John 9:1-12) Miracles. Miracle Territory. I have no idea how God will use this book. All I know is that it is HIS, not mine. And with Him all things are possible!

HOW IS IT POSSIBLE?

So, you may be asking how is it that we can make these changes and how is it possible to give up the foods that we have been raised eating? Is it truly what we are being called to do as Christians? First of all, making such a dramatic change is not something that a family can do "overnight". Most families live a very hectic lifestyle, we are homes of chaos—we pack too much into our day so that there is very little time left for pursuing God, prayer, Bible reading, devotions or taking the time to tap into our destinies or plan for our life, not to mention eating healthy foods. We are living mediocre, compromised lives.

Many Christians do not stop to think about God until some tragedy has occurred or they are in need of something financially! We are just too busy! Guilty as charged! That is why taking the time at the first of each year and making a decision to hear from God, to stop some of the turmoil and chaos and seek His direction is SO important in the world in which we live! Our boys were just 5 years and 12 years old when we began fasting and seeking God the first 21 days of the year. Fasting for them is part of their lives, they were raised this way, which is awesome and most likely one of the reasons they both love the Lord with all their hearts! But in spite of that our lives were still full of chaos and too much activity. I raised them on fast foods, microwaves and sugary breakfasts, just like most of the moms in the world today! And there was sickness. Lots of it!

Looking back, it seems that it should have been so clear to me what was going on with our bodies, but it was not—we were doing all we could do to "get by" just like most families are today, and we thought we were doing the best for our children that we could! One of my favorite scriptures is "my people are destroyed for lack of knowledge". More specifically, according to the NIV, *"My people are being destroyed because they don't know me. Since you priests refuse to know me, I refuse to recognize you as my priests. Since you have forgotten the laws of your God, I will forget to bless your children."* (Hosea 4:6) Wow! This is such a powerful scripture. Most often when we hear it, all we hear is the first part, "My people are being destroyed for lack of knowledge"—but take a look at the rest, and hear the power of it, "I will forget to bless your children." That is a powerful verse. When we are not obedient to God, He cannot bless our children, in other words, our children suffer because of our stupidity, our stubbornness! God showed me during this Fast that we are leading our children down a path of destruction in their health, and we are destroying our bodies every single day as we continue to put food in our mouths that are poison. The sad thing is, there is plenty of evidence out there that the food we eat every single day is, in fact, killing us, and yet because we are so weak in our flesh and in our spirit-man we don't deny our flesh and feed our spirits! We willingly walk down a path of destruction and we are teaching our children our same bad habits. We are creating a generation of sick children who will grow into sicker adults.

Read these statistics and I pray they will make you cringe in shame. According to the American Cancer Society, the average age of children being diagnosed with cancer is 6-years-old. The number one cause of death in children ages 14-16 (besides accidents) is cancer. 1 in 3 women will be diagnosed with cancer this year, 1 in 2 men. These statistics are staggering. And it doesn't matter whether we are talking about Christians or non-Christians—these are the facts. Cancer and disease have gotten so commonplace, so *expected* in our world today! We no longer bat an eye when our neighbor, our teacher, our friend is diagnosed with cancer, and yet according to the Bible and God's promises we are supposed to be living in abundance and health! Our altars are filled with people asking God for healing—and believe me, God IS in the miracle business. He heals today just as He healed when He walked the streets of Jerusalem. But, (and I am going to be bold here) He is weary of our prayers. He is weary of watching us day after day, year after year, eating the poison we call food and then wondering why we are sick. As Christians we truly are called to be set apart from the world, and more often than not a true Christian will abstain from sins that are accepted by the world as sin—we don't listen to bad music, we don't take our children to "R" rated movies, we don't partake in pornography or even drinking alcohol. And yet, every single day we still corrupt the temple that God gave us by eating poison. Just as Daniel had seen the effects that the king's meat had on the health of those who ate it, we KNOW it isn't good for us, so why is it so difficult to change?

Tracee Randall

ON MY SOAPBOX

I believe the answer to that question is because so much of our culture has been surrounded by the food we eat, and yes, even by the "feasts" that were so prevalent during the days of the Bible! When I go home to Louisiana for a visit, from the time I step foot into my Mom's home there is talk about what we are eating for lunch, what's for dinner and then what's for breakfast the next day. Our culture equates food with family—food is connected to every emotion that we experience, and it is used as a point of celebration from birthday cakes to marriage to death! Where people gather they bring food. I can imagine how Daniel and the other Hebrew boys must have felt when they sat at the king's table. Spread before them was every delicacy you could imagine. The richest meats, the most succulent desserts, a feast fit for a king! Imagine the temptation he must have felt to "give in" and eat from the king's table! He could have easily fallen into the lifestyle of those around him; he was away from his family, his culture, and suddenly thrust into an environment where no one would have known if he strayed from God's law and ate from the king's table. You can imagine today, going to a feast—a Thanksgiving spread that has all the goodies, all the delicacies and delicious foods that we can imagine, and saying, "No thank you" as Daniel did! It certainly must have been difficult, even with his convictions. It would have been so easy to give into the temptation because everyone else did! In Hebrews 4:16 it says that "He also provides strength for us to overcome temptation." I would agree that without tapping into God's strength it would be all but impossible to live a lifestyle of eating such as Daniel did. A lifestyle of fasting.

My family has been able to make those changes. I have already shared with you how my daughter-in-love, Katrina has made those changes for her family. That would include my son, Robby and our 3 grand-babies, Shalom who is 4, Mikhae'l who is 2 and Maryrose who will be 1 year old at the release of this book! As the Lord began to show her ways to use healthy food to help my son Robby's body heal, she realized that the only way to stay healthy was to make some serious changes, and she did it. If you can imagine this—Shalom just turned 4 years old in March of this year. We were invited to her Princess Birthday party—what do you see at any 4-year-old princess party?? Beautiful dresses, crowns, cupcakes, cookies, ice cream.....a big cake in the shape of a princess dress with lots of icing-roses and dots of chocolate for gem stones! But that is exactly the opposite of what Katrina served at Shalom's party. We had cut up fruit and veggies—we had a homemade treat made of dates and nuts that the children love! There were candles and gifts and laughter, just like any birthday party, but no sugar, no sweets, no kool-aid or even fruit juice boxes—only "God-made" food! And the really awesome thing about it is that no one missed the cake, no one missed the sugar! In my book, <u>Get MAD about Cancer</u>, I explain the hazards of drinking even 1 can of soda has on our immune system! At most parties there is so much sugar, so much junk that the kids are wired to the max and eventually get out of control. Their sensitive immune systems are weakened, and they are exposed to the germs from all the other children, it's no wonder that we see so much sickness and illness immediately after a party or family function! We blame it on the germs and being around other kids (same with daycare), which is true to some extent, but IF their immunes systems hadn't crashed with all that sugar and junk food, their bodies would be able to fight off the illness! Because of the decisions that our family has made, I can't remember the last time any of us had a cold, flu, or even a headache! Our wellness is a testimony to the truth that is shared in chapter 1 of Daniel—when we eat the right foods our bodies are stronger, healthier and our minds are sharper and clearer than anyone else's! Isn't this the promise that God has given us? An abundant life, free of sickness and disease!

What are the changes we have made and how? This is not an easy answer. I am working on other projects that will help families who are drawn to this book and who are drawn to this message of a fasting lifestyle to learn how to make those changes. I invite you to follow my blogs and my website as the Lord continues to give me creative ideas on how to spread this information to not just the church, but to those who do not know Him as well! With the Lord's help I will create a wellness program that will teach parents and grandparents how to raise healthy, strong children in a world that is literally dying! But, it isn't something that can be done overnight. My suggestion is to make 1 change per month and allow it to become a habit. I will give you an example: make a decision to fast sodas for 21 days. Drink only water and seek the Lord when you are tempted to drink one. Every time you resist the temptation, thank God for giving you the strength to do it. At the end of the 21 days, make the decision that you will do it again. Decide as a family that your health is the most important aspect of your lives, and explain to your children (no matter how young or old they are!) that you are going to make some changes so that they will live long, healthy lives, free of disease and pain! When you agree to do this as a family it is so much easier. (Contact me for more information about making healthy changes through my program, "50 Weeks & 50 New Habits"- Tracee@TraceeRandall.com)

My husband, Bobby was the hardest to change. He's a "typical man" and really thought that he had to have "meat and potatoes" at every meal, and he LOVES sweets! He didn't believe that he would have the energy he needed without eating meat, and he certainly did not want to 'give up' sweets for any period of time. When I told him at the beginning of this year that the Lord showed me that we were to live a lifestyle of fasting, and eat as Daniel did, he told me point blank that I could do it, but he wasn't going to. He continued to sneak candy and junk food into the house, but as he watched me change, as he watched our son Ryan (who is 21) change, he slowly began to make some changes too! Just small changes at first. We stopped drinking cow's milk and switched to Almond milk. In his lunch I packed lots of fruits and cut up veggies and hummus for dipping instead of traditional dips. He noticed that he had more energy and he began watching his belly shrink down. People began to ask him if he had lost weight, which he had, and he liked it! The most important thing though, is that we know we are healthy, we know that we have strong immune systems, we can fight off disease—and like Daniel, our minds are sharp and clear!

According to the Bible, and according to our pastor, "when you fast, you abstain from food for spiritual purposes." In Chapter 1 Daniel was not fasting. When the Bible talks about what Daniel ate it describes his *lifestyle*, and he was doing it because it was God's law. We certainly are no longer required by law to eat certain foods, or to abstain from certain foods. However, if you look at the foods that were forbidden to be eaten, these are the same foods that cause our bodies to be unhealthy! Coincidence? I don't believe it is!

As a wellness coach I have watched so many people die early deaths because they were not willing to make changes to their diets. Many of these people were "good people", Christians, people with a calling on their lives. Most of them died having still unfulfilled the true purpose that God had for them. Sickness and disease will cause people to lose their vision, to focus on themselves rather than be able to fulfill their true purpose and the plan that God has for them! Unfortunately we are padding the pockets of the doctors and hospitals because we are oblivious to the fact that our lifestyle is killing us! Taking medications has become acceptable for children of all ages, and rather than going back to the basics of what is at the root of these diseases, we accept the "magic pill" that covers the symptoms and causes more side effects than the disease itself! It's a vicious cycle. I believe that God is calling the church to rise up out of mediocrity, to set themselves apart from the world in this area! As children of God we must be strong, we must be healthy, we must have energy to fight the enemy who has come to "steal, kill and destroy." (John 10:10) Satan has laughed at us as Christians. How disrespectful for us to eat fast foods every day, the "king's meat" which causes stress on our digestive system, our hearts, our liver—and then when we have that heart attack ask God to heal us of our disease! It mocks God when we do this!

What if you went out into the busy highway and stood in the middle of the racing traffic? You could dodge a few cars for a while, but inevitably you will be hit, injured and taken to the hospital. The doctors patch you up, send you home, and you thank God for sparing your life. But then, the next day you go right back out into the center of the freeway, dodging the cars racing by, praying you won't get hit again! Would anyone believe that you deserved not to be hit? Would anyone expect God to spare you from being hit by the passing cars? Of course not. And yet, we do the very same thing with our health and our eating habits. Year after year we eat those foods that do not serve us well, we "play in the traffic" and suddenly one day, we are "hit" by that diagnosis—heart disease, diabetes, cancer. It brings us to our knees in prayer, "Lord, heal me," we plead. And we go to the doctor who prescribes this drug or that drug, patches us up and sends us back home. On the way home we stop and get ice cream to celebrate! At home there are decadent foods that well-meaning friends and church members have brought us to help us through our recovery! Nothing changes. And a year later it happens all over again, or worse, we die suddenly of a massive heart attack or stroke and everyone shakes their heads and talk about what a shame it happened to such a good man or woman! The Lord has clearly shown me during this fast that we as Christians must break that cycle of ignorance!

TAKE A STAND

We are living in a time when Christians are being persecuted and killed for their faith. There is a very real enemy in the world, and he has truly come to beat and persecute the Christians. It is time to take a stand for what we believe in, for our faith, and to stand on the Word of God and claim our victory over sickness and disease! The enemy enjoys watching us go to the altars praying to be healed. He loves watching us "eat, drink and be merry", and he is excited that the people of the church are as sick as the world! What a horrible example of God's miraculous power in us that we are living with disease on one hand and claiming God's healing power on the other! We must have strength in our bodies and in our spirits to fight the battles ahead for people in this end-time world we live in! When our flesh is weak, when we are sick, our spirits suffer too! When our bodies hurt, we cannot fight the enemy! Many Christians don't have energy enough to Fast, to pray, to worship! If we don't change, how can we expect to change the world?

Once we have made the decision to live a lifestyle of fasting, that is, eating in much the way Daniel ate—fresh fruits and raw veggies, God will give us the strength we need to do it! We are completely satisfied eating the way we eat! I carry my fruits and veggies and healthy snacks with me everywhere that I go, and made the decision that I will not live with the disease that others do. I am 55-years-old (almost 56!) and I feel amazing! I have no pain in my body at all! I have more energy than people ½ my age, and my skin is young looking and clear! I am on no medications and can't remember having a headache or stomach ache. No colds, no flus, no minor issues to *distract* me from the amazing plan that God has on my life! I am not perfect, but I make conscious decisions about what foods I choose to eat or not eat, and I feel that I am an example of what our lives can be if we make these changes! Our family memories are made around the table filled with fruits and delicious veggies, and it is no longer all about the food but more about our relationships and love for each other!

Perhaps the enemy has you so bound in fear that you don't believe you could possibly walk in the greatness of health that God has for you! I am here to tell you that you have bought into the lie of the enemy, and through FASTing God can give you wisdom to make changes that will impact your health for the better. (See the full disclosure statement at the front of this book regarding those who are in a physician's care). The Lord would have me say to you that whatever you BELIEVE about your circumstances is your reality. What you SPEAK about your health becomes your truth. I have worked with so many people who say to me, "I am sick, I have always been sick and the doctors say there is nothing I can do or they can do." When I hear this I cringe because the enemy has stolen hope from them! GOD can give you the wisdom to make healthy choices that can change everything for you, but YOU have to seek Him and be willing to believe and to make the changes.

Fasting is an incredible way to slow down our quick pace and allow ourselves time and quiet to hear God's voice. When we Fast we make a decision to "give up" the cravings and desires of our flesh, and to seek His power, His influence, His whisper and direction for our lives! If you have never fasted, I encourage you to start with a simple fast—fast 3 days. Dedicate this time to seeking God's direction—perhaps start with the traditional "Daniel Fast". No sweets, bread, meat or drinks other than water. For some even this Fast is a dramatic change from their normal lifestyle, but the great news is if you ask God to help you, the fasting part becomes easier. During this 3 days of fasting, I encourage you to read the chapter on fasting in the book of Daniel—according to Daniel 10:3- "I ate no pleasant *or* desirable food, nor did any meat or wine come into my mouth." After 3 weeks of prayer and dedication to God, 21 days—this is where we get the "21-Day Fast"—on the 21st day an angel appeared to Daniel and spoke these words to him, "Fear not, Daniel, for from the first day that you set your mind *and* heart to understand and to humble yourself before your God, your words were heard..." This is powerful. Fasting releases God's divine direction for our lives—through the angel that appeared to Daniel or through the still, small voice of God.

You will find after 3 days of fasting in this way that your mind is sharper, and although you may be a bit more hungry than usual, you will have more energy and feel better! But most importantly, you are being obedient to God's Word, which will open doors of blessing that no man can shut!

I know this short book is only a small portion of what you need to know to consider making this change—to begin a lifestyle of healthier eating and filling our temple with food that is honoring to God. I invite you to learn more by visiting my website. In my book titled <u>Get MAD about Cancer</u> I share more about how to make some changes that will help create a healthy lifestyle for your family! I also share valuable information about supplements and healthy alternatives that can help you—feel free to reach out to me about this—God has put this passion in my heart!

If you have never Fasted, ask God to reveal to you how to start—seek direction from a trusted pastor, connect with some of the literature on fasting, and contact me about how we've been able to tap into this incredible experience and draw closer to God! You will be amazed at the insights you will gain and how your relationship will be strengthened through this act of obedience! In his article, "9 Reasons For Fasting", Jentezen Franklin shares that "fasting will help us with freedom from addictions, for help with financial troubles, for national revival, for help with depression, major life decisions, health and healing, and for protection against danger." (http://jfm-website.s3.amazonaws.com/fasting/article/Nine-Reasons.pdf) I encourage you, seek God through fasting—it is the FASTest way to His favor and blessing on your life!

(Please go to my website, TraceeRandall.com and click on the icon that says "Subscribe to Receive Monthly Tips on how to walk in Miracle Territory in your Health"—these tips will help you make the changes necessary to live a healthier lifestyle!)

Romans 10:17 (KJV) "So then faith cometh by hearing, and hearing by the word of God."

CHAPTER 3

MORE FASTING TESTIMONIES

In a previous chapter I shared about some of the miracles that have happened to me this year following the 21-day first fruits fast. This is our 15th year with our church in fasting, and as you can imagine we truly have had some amazing miracles occur within our family as a direct result of fasting. Each year our family sits down together and we create a list of prayer requests, needs in our lives for salvation for our family, for healing, for addictions, and financial needs. (In the back of the book you will find a area to write down your prayer requests and what prayers and needs that you will ATTACH to your FAST.) God has ALWAYS answered our prayers, always. For many years our ongoing prayer request was for the healing of our son, Robby, who was born with a serious skin condition that literally controlled our lives for many years. He has been healed of this affliction, and God has shown us through changing our lifestyle of eating how our bodies are designed to *heal themselves.* I would like to share some other testimonies and other insights that have occurred when we fasted as a family, and also share some of the testimonies of other family members and friends who I know God has used mightily in the kingdom. I pray that these testimonies will raise your faith, will help you see the power when we combine prayer with fasting, and when we seek God will all of our hearts!

According to the Bible, there are some things that simply cannot be prayed away, it takes adding FASTING to the mix! Let me share in Mark 9 what happened with a boy who was possessed by an evil spirit. The disciples had tried to cast out the demon, but nothing was happening. Here's what happened when Jesus entered the picture (notice the final verse):

Mark 9: 1-29 (KJV)

"9 And he said unto them, Verily I say unto you, That there be some of them that stand here, which shall not taste of death, till they have seen the kingdom of God come with power.

² And after six days Jesus taketh with him Peter, and James, and John, and leadeth them up into an high mountain apart by themselves: and he was transfigured before them.

³ And his raiment became shining, exceeding white as snow; so as no fuller on earth can white them.

⁴ And there appeared unto them Elias with Moses: and they were talking with Jesus.

⁵ And Peter answered and said to Jesus, Master, it is good for us to be here: and let us make three tabernacles; one for thee, and one for Moses, and one for Elias.

⁶ For he wist not what to say; for they were sore afraid.

⁷ And there was a cloud that overshadowed them: and a voice came out of the cloud, saying, This is my beloved Son: hear him.

⁸ And suddenly, when they had looked round about, they saw no man any more, save Jesus only with themselves.

⁹ And as they came down from the mountain, he charged them that they should tell no man what things they had seen, till the Son of man were risen from the dead.

¹⁰ And they kept that saying with themselves, questioning one with another what the rising from the dead should mean.

¹¹ And they asked him, saying, Why say the scribes that Elias must first come?

¹² And he answered and told them, Elias verily cometh first, and restoreth all things; and how it is written of the Son of man, that he must suffer many things, and be set at nought.

¹³ But I say unto you, That Elias is indeed come, and they have done unto him whatsoever they listed, as it is written of him.

¹⁴ And when he came to his disciples, he saw a great multitude about them, and the scribes questioning with them.

¹⁵ And straightway all the people, when they beheld him, were greatly amazed, and running to him saluted him.

¹⁶ And he asked the scribes, What question ye with them?

¹⁷ And one of the multitude answered and said, Master, I have brought unto thee my son, which hath a dumb spirit;

¹⁸ And wheresoever he taketh him, he teareth him: and he foameth, and gnasheth with his teeth, and pineth away: and I spake to thy disciples that they should cast him out; and they could not.

¹⁹ He answereth him, and saith, O faithless generation, how long shall I be with you? how long shall I suffer you? bring him unto me.

²⁰ And they brought him unto him: and when he saw him, straightway the spirit tare him; and he fell on the ground, and wallowed foaming.

²¹ And he asked his father, How long is it ago since this came unto him? And he said, Of a child.

²² And ofttimes it hath cast him into the fire, and into the waters, to destroy him: but if thou canst do any thing, have compassion on us, and help us.

²³ Jesus said unto him, If thou canst believe, all things are possible to him that believeth.

²⁴ And straightway the father of the child cried out, and said with tears, Lord, I believe; help thou mine unbelief.

²⁵ When Jesus saw that the people came running together, he rebuked the foul spirit, saying unto him, Thou dumb and deaf spirit, I charge thee, come out of him, and enter no more into him.

²⁶ And the spirit cried, and rent him sore, and came out of him: and he was as one dead; insomuch that many said, He is dead.

²⁷ But Jesus took him by the hand, and lifted him up; and he arose.

[28] And when he was come into the house, his disciples asked him privately, Why could not we cast him out?

[29] And he said unto them, 'This kind can come forth by nothing, but by prayer and fasting.'"

There are some things that we cannot change except by FASTING- Fasting gets God's attention. This is a powerful story that explains the power of fasting! We also see the same story in Matthew 17—a man comes up to Jesus and bows down to Him asking Him to cure his son who has been possessed by a demon. He tells Jesus that the disciples could not heal or cure him! Jesus casts the demonic spirit out of the boy. When they have him alone, the disciples ask Jesus why they were not able to cure the boy. Jesus answers in verse 20 of Matthew 17, '"Because of the littleness of your faith; for truly I say to you, if you have faith the size of a mustard seed, you will say to this mountain, 'Move from here to there,' and it will move; and nothing will be impossible to you.[21] "But this kind does not go out except by prayer and fasting.'"

What an incredible example of the power of FASTing. What Jesus was saying is that there are just some things that cannot be cured or healed or delivered without FASTing first! There are generational curses in our families that we must FAST for! There are bondages that must be broken off of people's lives, addictions, sickness—and the Bible tells us that there is POWER in FASTing!

I asked my son Robby, the son who was born with that dreadful disease, the son who has been "on fire" for the Lord since he first set foot into our church over 18 years ago, the son who has been chosen by God to take the love of Christ and the "Good News" of the gospel into all the nations to share his thoughts on fasting:

Tracee Randall

"Fasting" by Robby Randall

"There is an appetite for God. And it can be awakened. I invite you to turn from the dulling effects of food and the dangers of idolatry, and to say with some simple fast: 'This much, O God, I want you.'" (John Piper, Desiring God.org)

Fasting has never been an easy thing for me. Each and every time I decide to fast, no matter how long it is, it always comes with a sense of anxiety. Instantly, the moment I set my mind to fast I begin to crave foods that I have not even thought of in months. Enchiladas smothered in melting cheese, fresh sushi dipped in spicy mayo sauce and a breakfast burrito filled with sautéed red onions, green peppers, pepper jack cheese and fluffy scrambled eggs. And as in a normal day, full of *to-do lists* and mundane responsibilities, accidentally skipping a meal goes unnoticed, but simply one hour into a fast and my stomach is gripped with the pangs of childbirth and my brain is convinced I am going to starve.

But despite the said obstacles, I try and make fasting a regular part of my life; you could even say I try to make it my lifestyle. There are many ideas and philosophies about the topic of fasting, but for me personally, I have seen fasting as a practical way to humble myself before the Lord.

There are many promises made to those who come to God in true humility. One verse that strikes me the most is, James 4:6, *"God opposes the proud but gives grace to the humble."* I don't know about you, but when I read this verse I do not want to be found as one qualifying for the first part. In fact, I am motivated by this verse to do everything in my power to fit into the latter half. Having three small children present enough challenges as it is, I have no need to add being *opposed by God* into my life.

Dictionary.com defines *pride* as an *inordinate opinion of one's own dignity, importance, merit, or superiority.* When we view ourselves, our opinions, our morals, our values, our passions, as higher than Jesus or the things He defines as valuable and important, then we find ourselves as a people like the Jews in the Old Testament, for God said, *"I have seen this people, and indeed it is a stiff-necked people!"*

Though I am not perfect and would not even stand a chance for the *Most Humble Person in the World* award, I do make it my aim to continuously grow in humility before God. Over the years intentionally fasting has been one of the most effective mechanisms to remind me of my great need for Jesus and His strength. As Isaiah said in chapter 51, "...you have forgotten the LORD your Maker, Who stretched out the heavens and laid the foundations of the earth..." It is so easy as life gets fuller and fuller that we tend to forget that we are only frail, weak humans that need the grace and might of our Creator and Redeemer.

Every time I choose to fast food for any amount of time, my physical hunger comes as a reminder that I would surely die without God blessing me with every single breath. The realization of this truth draws my heart to a posture of being bowed low and fills my mouth again with prayers of thanksgiving. And as I am prone to trust in my own strength, I need something in my life to anchor me to my undeniable need for God. Fasting regularly has served me as this anchor.

But fasting comes in many colors and flavors. As a spiritual discipline it is choosing to abstain from anything that is part of your regular routine; including food, Facebook, Twitter, Instagram, movies, TV, music, watching the news or whatever you choose.

I have engaged with many styles of fasting over the years, but in 2006, I did my first entertainment/media fast.

Imagine three months with no movies, no news reports, no blogs or Facebook statuses, no tweets or retweets, no video games and no music of any kind except worship. After about three days my mind was telling me I was crazy, that I was going to miss out on life. But I knew it had to be done. I needed to detox the distractions around me. I filled my time with spending time with Jesus, reading the Bible and worship. After the three months my life was completely changed. My mind was clearer. My devotion was stronger. And the best part was that I didn't NEED media any more. In fact, I mostly lost my appetite for it. Instead I experienced a new and deeper hunger for God like never before. I had developed a love for the Word of God that was more satisfying than anything else I had tasted. To this day fasting has been a regular part of my life and I would not be the man I am today without this great, yet terrible, discipline.

    Robby Randall RobbyRandall.com

*****

I also asked my good friend Destiny Yarbrough to share anything that God laid on her heart that fasting has done for her. Destiny is happily married to Wes Yarbrough and they are the proud parents of a truly blessed 13 year old son, Spencer. Destiny has been serving Christ for over 13 years, serving on ministry teams, leading small groups, local outreach by way of feeding the homeless, hosting women's conferences and ministry counseling.

After a painful divorce with her previous husband who battled with addiction, God gave her the passion and desire to help other hurting women through her testimony and life experiences and because of this "Daughters of Deliverance Ministries and Hope" was birthed. The vision is to help women encounter God through inspiration, words of encouragement, education, empowerment and mentoring. Giving hope through the power and blood of Jesus Christ. Here's what she shared:

"In the midst of a devastating separation which eventually led to a divorce from my ex-husband battling with a drug and alcohol addiction dependency, I had to depend on God to comfort and guide me on what to do. Fasting is so important when making major life-changing decisions and it brings you so much closer to God. Through fasting and prayer, God will show you the secret things and He reveals so much to you in the spirit.

During this time I had no other choice but to fast and pray and seek God for guidance on what to do and what decisions to make regarding my situation. I had a child to think of as well.

I prayed specific prayers and gave it all to God. I prayed for God to save my marriage and to change my ex-husband's desire to medicate through drugs and alcohol, but God had a much bigger and better plan for my son and me!

God spoke to me boldly and He walked me through this time as He protected my son and me through the fire. He gave me a new strength that I did not have on my own.

I believe in fasting and prayer and I am a living testimony as to what God CAN DO. There is a rainbow at the end of the story. I have remarried to a Christian man who is a wonderful father to my son, and a good husband to me. God has restored what the enemy tried to take from me and has blessed me with a new beginning.

My fasting led to breakthrough, increase, favor and trust in Him!"

DESTINY YARBROUGH

There is another amazing woman who attends our church that I highly respect and I know she and her husband are very strong Christians and have fasted for many years. Here is what she wrote about fasting:

"What you think makes up the ingredients, or formula for fasting, may not be what it is at all. There can be physical, medical, and/or spiritual aspects of fasting. You can use one approach or combine any of the 3. One aspect of fasting that you should consider is fasting for spiritual reasons. When fasting spiritually, one eats dirt! Yes, I said "Dirt!"

2 Chronicles 20:18 'And Jehosaphat bowed his head with his face to the ground; and all Judah and the inhabitants of Jerusalem fell before the Lord, worshipping the Lord.'

Again and again hit the deck of dirt....fasting!

When fasting, remember to take high quality protein, liquid and/or powder. Your heart is a muscle that needs protein, especially when fasting. Make a simple, clear list of what you expect for yourself during your fast. It can be a prayer that needs to be answered. It could be physical pounds lost. You can read about and learn the benefits of fasting in articles on the internet and there are many books on the subject of fasting.

Fasting can make you very sensitive to your surroundings, odors, tastes, feelings of others, and it can help you gain insight for you and for others. Here is an example. Myself and a colleague had been fasting for a women's leadership conference. While fasting, Tracee asked me to write a fasting testimony. Because I was fasting, I was alert in my senses. At about the same time my husband called and told me that I couldn't come home at that moment, there had been a gas leak that had shut down our entire community.

That was my signal from God to stop my world, stop my daily routine and focus on this topic of fasting.

When you fast you will receive many benefits, both spiritual and physical. Send Tracee feedback about how you benefit from fasting! Fasting improves your health, and will inspire others to do the same!

Sandy's Testimony

So many amazing miracles have happened for our family as a direct result of FASTING. One of the most inspiring is what happened in 2003 for our nephew David and his mom, Sandy.

After the sudden death of David's father Bill, Sandy began a spiral downward that included severe depression, panic attacks and hopelessness. Left with 2 young sons to raise alone, she sought medical attention and was prescribed anti-depressants and the potent and addictive pain killer oxycodone to relieve some back pain. She found that the drugs numbed her hurt, too and very quickly she was taking 5-10 pills per day and her drug habit grew daily. David was an impressionable 12-year-old, and easily fell prey to the drugs in his neighborhood. Although Sandy hid her secret VERY well, David was not so cautious. Thankfully he was arrested after a party at his home got out of control, and because of his age and recent passing of his father, we were allowed to take him into our custody, and Bobby drove the long road to Memphis from Atlanta prepared to bring an angry young man home with him.

After much heartache, struggle, prayer, fasting, and determination— shedding many tears, David was miraculously delivered, saved & set free during a Sunday night service at our church. We watched this young man blossom from an angry, hurt, "mad at God" teenager to an on-fire, radical, leader in the youth group-- on fire for Christ!

It was a few weeks after this that he shared the secret of his mother's addiction and begged us to help him set her free as well. We all knew that it had to be God for this transformation to occur, and began praying for an answer. With just a few weeks left before summer was over and school would start back, we devised a plan to get her here to spend a weekend with David. Then we went to work--- FASTING. For the 21 days prior to her arrival, all of us-- David, my husband Bobby, our sons Robby & Ryan all agreed to seek God through FASTING. We put scriptures on notecards & hung them throughout the house. We did communion together every morning & intently sought the Lord, each in our own way. We knew that this could only be broken through FASTING & as the days grew closer the enemy did his best to sabotage our plan. Oxycodone is one of the most addictive, harmful drugs on the market. David educated us on the withdrawal effects of coming off this type of drug, not to mention Sandy's anger and pain she was medicating with this addiction.

Finally she arrived on a Friday. Our plans were to go to Stone Mountain as a family on Saturday, take her to church Sunday morning and she was driving back to Memphis Sunday night to be at work on Monday morning. Well, that›s what we told her. But we were diligently praying and FASTING that God would intervene SOMEHOW on Sunday morning.

David told us that she had brought enough drugs to last through Sunday night. He was afraid of what would happen if she stopped cold-turkey, but we just kept our faith!

Sunday morning we were feeling that God was about to move and our hearts were full. We sat through the incredible service, and then the altar call! The Holy Spirit moved and we watched Sandy make the long walk to the altar. I followed her down instinctively. She prayed with an altar worker and then I tapped her on the shoulder...."we know about the drugs" I whispered. She desperately tried to deny it but God was working on her. She burst into tears and began sobbing, asking God, David, us to forgive her. We told her we had been fasting for 21-days for deliverance and we believed that God would help her get free.

Sandy has a nursing background and although she wanted desperately to be delivered from the chains of addiction, she knew the risk of stopping cold turkey. She was in no shape to drive home, so we agreed to return to church for the night service and ask God for direction.

That afternoon we talked about how she had fallen into this lifestyle, we set a plan to help her, and waited on God. She told us that if she didn't have an oxycodone by noon the next day she would begin a horrible detox. There would be sweats and chills and nausea and vomiting and pain. Sometimes the heart would stop. She said she had never seen someone come off them without intervention.

God however, had different plans. We went to church that evening and the pastor gave a WORD that struck her to the core and we watched her writhe in the altar in true repentance.

God completely showed off. Our church announced a camp meeting and the next 3 nights the Holy Spirit would fall on our church.

The detox was horrible. Sandy sweated buckets of water then would wrap herself in blankets unable to find warmth, shivering uncontrollably. She writhed on the floor in pain, screaming for help--she would monitor her heart and assure us she wasn't dying-- this was part of the process. We threw her in the shower every afternoon and made the 45-minute drive to our church & God always showed up!!

At the end of the third day she walked out of our bedroom and said calmly, "it's done."

That was 10 years ago. God is faithful. So faithful.

Today Sandy is an amazing woman who has worked hard to take care of her younger son, Daniel, and provide a home for him that is free from the drug abuse and alcohol addictions that had plagued her for so many years. She has a heart for the Lord, she is free from self-condemnation and free from the bondage the enemy had her wrapped in for many years. She is free. We KNOW she is free because of the FASTING and prayer that we covered her in—there was nothing nor no one that could have broken the hold the enemy had on her, and as a result the generational curse of addiction has also been broken off of her 2 boys. David is happily married now and he and his beautiful wife are expecting their first baby! God is so good. We are so grateful for our church, our pastor, and to God for the blessing He is pouring out on our family!

*****

I have mentioned my incredible daughter-in-love, Katrina several times in this book. Her dedication, sensitive spirit, and love for the Lord shines through in every aspect of her life. She is raising (along with my son Robby) some incredibly anointed and dedicated children to the Lord and I respect her as a true example of a Proverbs 31 woman. Married to Robby at the tender age of 21, she has grown into an amazing woman of God. I have learned much from this woman. I love her as if she were my own daughter, and am grateful for the love she has given my son, for the way she raises my G-babies, and for who she is! Here's what Katrina has to say about fasting:

"Fasting" by Katrina Randall

"I came to the Lord at a young age between 7-10 years old. My immediate family was divorced, remarried, alcoholic, addicted to drugs, and very resistant to the Gospel message. Despite all that, my grandfather introduced me to Jesus and began to take me to church when I was about 5 years old. The first church I ever attended was an old, traditional, Southern, Spirit-filled church that flowed in all the gifts. I soon got saved and began speaking in tongues by the time I was 12. Because I was the only Christian in my immediate household, I didn't have much access to discipleship besides, "Read your Bible and pray."

I was 18 years old when I was first introduced to fasting, intercession, evangelism, Bible-study, accountability and living a holy, righteous lifestyle. At this time in my life I was young, single, fearless and hungry for the deep things of God. I immediately dived into fasting in an extreme way. Water fasting, juice fasting, Daniel fasting....for 3 days, 10 days, 21 days, 40 days—you name it! I've done it all. And it was glorious! I would not be the woman I am today without the years I spent fasting and praying in this way. But, those are not the stories I want to tell today. I want to tell the story of how fasting has impacted my life as a young mother.

I got married when I was 21 years old and still in the midst of my extreme pursuit of the Lord through fasting. We soon decided as a couple that we wanted to give the Lord complete control over when we got pregnant and how many children we would have. This would change my approach to fasting dramatically. You see, it's very difficult to do any kind of intense fast when you are pregnant, nursing or could become pregnant at any moment. I was actually in the middle of a 21-day liquid fast when I miscarried our first child because I wasn't yet aware that I was even pregnant when I began the fast.

I decided from then on that I needed to embrace a different kind of fasted lifestyle. A long-term marathon form of fasting over decades verses short term sprints of fasting. This was the only way I would be able to safely fast during my current life circumstance of pregnancy and nursing.

The change was very difficult for me at first. All I had known and experienced was the intense water fasting, the epic 40 days of pouring out my weakness before the Lord and crying out for breakthrough! I was deceived into thinking that any other type of fasting was pathetic and not legitimate before the Lord. But I didn't want to give up fasting altogether just because I had become a mother! I just needed to find a different approach.

My husband and I decided on 2 simple things to create a fasted lifestyle that was conducive to our entire family at every stage of life—all the way from conception to when they grow up and leave our home.

1. Our entertainment would come from God and each other.
2. Our nourishment and physical appetite would be satisfied by the things that God designed in nature for our bodies to live and thrive from.

We have now implemented these things into our family over the past 5 yrs. It has been a progressive thing that is always morphing and changing according to His leadership and insight into this lifestyle. We've had to repent often for being legalistic and for falling short in the convictions He has given us. And we are so aware of how much we still have to learn and grow on our level of consecration and dedication to Him in this particular avenue of fasting.

We now have 3 beautiful children....and the wisdom of this lifestyle is already bearing so much fruit in all of our lives. We do not have a TV or video games in our home, so our kids have vibrant and bright imaginations. They are so content in being entertained by each other, reading a book, cleaning the house with mom or running an errand with dad. Our days are mostly filled with interactions with each other, dancing, playing games, wrestling, answering all their many questions and playing dress up recitals of their favorite Bible stories. This has created fertile ground for rich, authentic and deep relationship with each other.

We decided not to bring junk-food into our home and to purchase only whole foods that bring true nourishment to the body. Our kids have never experienced fast-food, soft drinks, candy, etc. As a result, we all have such rich appetites! We fully delight ourselves in abundance of fruits, veggies, nuts, dates, carrot juice—all the wonderful things that God has designed for our bodies to consume and digest. We satisfy our palates with His creation and are genuinely uninterested in the things offered at birthday parties, Sunday school class and restaurants. Rarely is anyone ever sick, feverish or in pain. Except, of course, for the occasional discomforts that come with pregnancy, teething, mosquito bites and scraped knees.

In all this, we have grown so much in our relationship with the Lord and each other. And we have reached a level of wholeness and healing in our bodies that we never thought possible. Money could not have purchased these precious things for us. But the diligence and persistence of a slow and steady fasted lifestyle truly has given us these things in a measure far greater than we could have ever hoped or asked for."

Katrina Randall

There is an incredible man who is part of our church family at Free Chapel. Myraio Mitchell is one of the most Godly men I know—he has raised his family to serve the Lord and has a very humble spirit as well. Recently I learned more about the incredible faith legacy that his mother and father left him, and have come to respect him even more. I knew that after years of serving the Lord and Fasting he would have more than one testimony of a Fasting miracle, and asked him to share one for us here:

FAST of 2010 by Myraio L. Mitchell, Sr.

In 2004 after going through Chapter 13 bankruptcy for the 2nd time a year prior, but having experienced the favor with God through what was scheduled to be a 5-year repayment plan through the courts to pay a percentage to all creditors. God honored our faithfulness even after filing bankruptcy, and we desired to re-pay our creditors. He was still faithful through it all. After 3 years of autodraft payments directly to the courts we received a statement in the mail. That day I received a call at work around lunch time from Shera, my wife, after she read the monthly statement that reflected our account was zero balance PAID IN FULL. I immediately wanted to call the courts because I believed it was a huge mistake and I didn't want to go to jail or have more of my wages garnished for missing a payment. I did call the court and to my amazement a young lady pulled the file number and verified this debt was indeed canceled of a balance over $12 thousand dollars remaining according to the original payment plan. We were a one-car family and needed another vehicle but we vowed not to buy another one and make-do with the one we had, we didn't want to add more sorrow to the financial situation or get deeper into debt after the miracle of God eliminating a bankruptcy debt. Who ever heard of such?!

During the 21-Day Fast of January 2010 on a Saturday morning I was at my "breaking point" once again. I was angry with God and detesting every outcome of every decision I was making and was seeking God's direction like never before. In desperation I went to the church and I was drawn to the altar to pray and just be open and honest with God. I did, and really poured out my true feelings and everything that was inside of me--the good, bad and indifferent. In addition to that I was very hungry because of committing to do a total fast for 14 days.

After going to work I received a call around 12 that afternoon from a couple that wanted to take my family and me to lunch. At the time my wife, Shera, known as "The Mary Kay Lady", was on a weekend retreat and the kids were home doing weekend chores. I told the couple we were not available that weekend. After declining, my "religious" mind kicked in and being the "fasting police" my family demes me as, and I thought, "We're fasting, why are they want to go out to eat?"

I continued to work and around 1:30PM my phone rang again. It was another call from the couple. I answered the phone "Hello, this is Myraio," and the lady asked, "Are you still working?" I said, "Yes ma'am I am." She then said, "Can you come and open the door for us? We just stopped by to see you for a brief moment."

I went to let them in. It was great to see them but in my mind I was thinking, "Why are they here and didn't I say we were not available to do lunch?" The husband proceeded to say, "We won't hold you up but we had to get this to you today." Still confused, I remember thinking, "OK, and what's this about so I can get back to work so I can pick up everyone by 7:30PM." He proceeded to say, "In this envelope is a title of that car parked outside." He pointed to a car parked in the lot and handed me a set of keys with the title. Then he said, "We had everything checked, and replaced major parts and new tires to included and detailed." I didn't know whether to cry, laugh, run, scream or what, so I did it all! I asked the gentleman's wife if this is how women feel when they are emotional. My heart was racing, pounding as if it was about to explode! My hands were shaking uncomfortably that I could barely hold the keys. You must understand, nothing like this had ever happened to me/us and to receive 2 life-changing miracles...BUT GOD could only do something of this magnitude.

Ok so, 5 hours earlier I was in "drama mode" with God and yet He was, I believe, laughing and just shaking His head and told my angels to "keep moving he's just venting." Everything on the previous vehicle we lost to repossession He gave back. Four door sport family vehicle, with Sunroof and etc... But this time it was a blessing not a curse.

See, we don't really understand what a blessing is. The blessings of the Lord makes a person rich and He adds no sorrow. What does this mean; when God blesses you there's no strings attached. When He blesses you there's no repayment plan. When He blesses you there's no APR (Annual Percentage Rate). When He blesses you there no agreement to sign. When He blesses you there's no loan officer needed. When He blesses you there's no credit check. When He blesses you its "zero down", "zero per month" and "no interest" for the remaining of the blessing!!! Come on somebody say "Amen" to this!!! Aren't you glad we have a God that's non-judgmental and has our best interest in mind at all times?

I Corinthian 2:14 – The person without the Spirit does not accept the things that come from the Spirit of God but considers them foolishness, and cannot understand them because they are discerned only through the Spirit.

No deviation, no discrepancy, just direction.

When we walk in the Spirit we can judge all things, but all things can judge us. We are operating on another level.

When we have divine orders from the Father it does not matter what anyone say or how they treat us. They are operating in their natural senses...see, smell, touch, hear and not the Spirit. So, don't waste time trying to debate or change their mind. They are undeveloped in areas spiritually that's why they get angry, upset and talk about people of spiritual nature "they are too spiritual". I Corinthians 12:1 says "I will not have you ignorant concerning Spiritual things". Begin to operate into another dimension...the Spirit realm. Many are saved, but ignorant spiritually. They want to be or are in a position of authority, but ignorant in "people skills" and business matters. Our lives are a direct reflection of what spirit we listen to. No one can stop what God called us to do; Jonah is a great example. Ephesians 1:7-8

Our lives at home, in the work place, or on the streets we strive/live on receiving and giving insight and wisdom to others from the Holy Spirit which is our GPS of life.

Myraio L. Mitchell, Sr.

Luke 18:1 "Then Jesus told his disciples a parable to show them that they should always pray and not give up."

CHAPTER 4

A LIFETIME OF FASTING— A TESTIMONY TO GOD'S FAITHFULNESS— ROBBY'S STORY

I watched as our son, Robby danced in the aisle of our church on Sunday night. His lanky arms and legs were like those of a puppet, flaying this way and that, worshipping in true abandonment before the Lord. My eyes filled with tears as I watched, he was lost in his worship, and unaware that I was watching every move he made, intently praying that God would heal his body. I closed my eyes for a moment to allow a few tears to escape and form tiny salty streams down my cheeks, stop for a moment on my chin, and then fall to the floor silently. I opened them again and smiled. My son. The other kids were dancing around him, all oblivious of each other, laughing and smiling and enjoying the freedom of worship that our church allowed on Sunday nights from its youth. A dozen or so of them made their way into the altars, still dancing and prancing and loving the Lord with all their hearts. Robby was caught up in it, and for that, I was so grateful.

I had watched our son suffer physically and mentally for too many years. He was 14-years-old and although we KNEW that God could heal his body of the disease that had plagued him since childhood, He had not yet done it, so we were just standing in prayer that tonight would be the night! Robby had been born with a severe rash that covered his body at birth—after many hours of intense labor, an umbilical cord that was strangling him with each push, and an exhausted decision by the doctors to perform an emergency C-Section, our beautiful son was covered with a rash that concerned us. The doctor wrote it off that it would go away, that he would 'grow out of it', and sent us home with our otherwise healthy baby boy. Robby's circumstances surrounding his conception were indeed not the best, and the entire story of it is shared in another work, but suffice it to say that had it not been for my conviction and fear of the Lord, (what little I knew of Him), Robby would most likely have been a victim of abortion at worst, or adoption at best. But here he was, 14-years-old, dancing before the Lord with wild abandonment, much like David as he paraded through the streets, not caring what others thought of his behavior!

That rash had never gone away as the doctor had promised, but instead it had continued to worsen, to the point that it covered his entire body from head to toe—we watched Robby writhe in pain scratching and itching day and night, night and day. Of course we had done everything possible medically, and then nutritionally and when nothing worked we had all but given up when we were invited to attend a church 45 minutes north of our home, in Gainesville, Georgia. Robby had been somewhat of an outcast in school—the rash caused him to be disruptive in class—as he was always scratching or trying not to scratch. The kids can be so cruel, and there was the fear of it spreading or someone "catching" it, so Robby was "hands off" in most circles. The disease had gotten so bad at this point, that we could no longer touch or hug him without him flinching away in pain, and just the gentle touch on any area of his body would cause an intense itching and scratching episode. It was at this church that we learned about a God who heals. It was also at this incredible church that it didn't really matter what was going on with Robby's skin—these kids danced together and loved the Lord—and it seemed that no matter what issues they were facing there was less judgement in this circle.

The youth pastor was amazing, Robby loved him, and he proved to be a mentor for Robby to look up to. When the youth announced that there would be a youth trip to Florida, to attend a big youth conference there, we were excited to allow Robby to attend. He went for the weekend and we were thrilled that he was finding a place for himself. I will never forget the night he returned home. Something about him was very different. We didn't know what it was back then, but today in hindsight I realize it was the "anointing", the "calling" that God had on his life that had changed him. It was while he was on that youth trip that an amazing prophetic word was spoken over him.

He told us about how there were hundreds of people there—mostly youth and youth pastors—churches from all over the country who had come together for this big meeting, and how he had gone to the altar to dance and worship with hundreds of other kids—flooding the aisles and altars—arms raised, tears flowing, the spirit of the Lord was moving. The music was playing, the musicians and singers praising loudly, when suddenly the pastor stopped everything. Robby told us how he had been called up on stage and how that pastor had spoken words over him and how it was prophetic. He couldn't remember exactly what had been said, but he excitedly told us that it had been videotaped and that we could purchase the video and watch the whole thing!

I could hardly wait, and with trembling hands I remember putting the tape in the VCR, pushing "play" and waiting for the words that had been spoken over my son. It was exactly as Robby had described. Hundreds of people, kids in blue shirts, yellow shirts, all representing the youth group of the church they attended—many of them in the altar, and there was Robby, standing at the foot of the stage, arms outstretched widely, his back to the camera, surrounded by kids that were bumping and pushing against him—as kids that age do at a rock concert! Suddenly, without warning, the pastor began to shout into the crowd, "Whose son is this?"

And it became apparent that he was speaking to Robby. The music all but stopped and you heard the pastor's voice again ask, "Whose son is this?"

Robby answered, "I'm on a youth trip."

Robby was ushered onto the stage to stand a few feet away from the man of God who was sitting on a tall stool, sweat stained his jacket and he held a large handkerchief as he was wiping the sweat from his eyes and face as he spoke.

"Oh—you're on a youth trip—oh! " he mopped his face and chuckled almost to himself. "I wish your parents were here to hear this—cause they don't know who they've raised. You don't even realize who you are yet. All you know is that you've got to stay with Jesus at all costs cause it hasn't even been revealed to you yet what God's about to do in you. Brother, you're about to enter into your purpose."

The music started again loudly and Robby stood trembling, arms raised before this man of God. His youth pastor stood behind him, weeping openly as this prophesy was spoken.

"For the anointing is on you." He paused, as if to allow this to sink into Robby's spirit. "In spite of all, you've been chosen by God. Yeah- in spite of your situation and environment you've been chosen by God." He raised his voice, "Your failures can't cancel you out, son. You haven't even begun to live yet. He's about to thrust you into a level of living---" Another pause as if he was listening for the word of the Lord.

"You are going to be like and unto a Joseph in your family. Oh my God! Even at a young age you're gonna have to suffer. But brother, at the end of that suffering, you're going to be the catalyst that saves your family. Raise your hands, boy!" He was shouting now, the music was playing in the background as if to accentuate his words.

"I feel the anointing..."

"You've made the right trip brother, you've made the right trip. Let Him put it in you. Let Him put it in your belly--- cause out of your belly's gonna flow rivers of living water! Somebody give God a shout of praise!"

"I feel the presence of God so thick in this place—somebody has prepared this atmosphere for this. The presence of God has been made to feel welcome in this place." And the music cascaded loudly, the drums, the cymbals and suddenly the entire room was in an uproar of praise and worship, with Robby lying trembling on the stage in front of this man of God, trembling and crying and feeling the anointing of God surrounding him like a huge warm blanket.

We watched this video over and over and over again. Even today, nearly 16 years later, I can hear the voice of the pastor, the tempo of the music, I can see Robby receiving his calling. What an incredible blessing.

We would watch the video and try to figure out what it meant. What did it mean "at a young age you're gonna have to suffer?" Why did he have to suffer? How would he "save his family?"

I would ask God these same questions at the beginning of each year. It seemed that with our commitment to fasting came the intimate relationship with God to be able to just ask whatever is on our hearts. We would sit around the table on the Saturday before the fast (which usually began the first Sunday in January each year) and begin to share our dreams, our prayers, our gratitude for what the Lord had already done. We were told to attach our fast to certain prayers, so that as we fasted and sought the Lord, He would give us direction or prayers would somehow miraculously be answered.

During our first fast, our #1 prayer was that Robby would be miraculously healed of this dreadful disease that caused him so much pain. We had a short list of other prayer requests too- for salvation for a nephew, a financial blessing in our business—but we all knew that the number 1 prayer, the number 1 miracle would be that of Robby's healing.

Our first 21-day fast was not easy. The excitement wore off by the 3rd day when we were hungry and our bodies were craving the foods we had set aside, and the mental part of it was much worse than the physical. Our pastor calls it "King Stomach"—the ruler of our flesh—but by God's grace we made it! Our youngest son, Ryan, who was 5 years old at the time, fasted sugar—no desserts on Sunday after church, no candy or ice-cream. He was happy to fast vegetables, but of course that was not an option. Robby did the "Daniel Fast" as did I, but Bobby opted to do a 3-day full fast at the beginning and at the end of the 21-day fast. I will never forget when, on the 19th day of the fast there was a bowl of bananas on the counter that had gotten a bit ripe and were creating that odor that an "overripe" banana has, and I threatened to throw them away if someone didn't eat them. Bobby had just started the full fast, which meant only water and some occasional juice or broth, but he insisted I keep them so that he could eat one on the morning after the fast was officially over. The thought of 3 more days smelling those rotten bananas was NOT appealing to me, but I consented to leave them there, waiting for him to dive in the moment the fast was completed!

The fast ended and the next morning I woke up to the smell of bacon and eggs being fried in a skillet on the stove, and laughed out loud as the 3 bananas were securely still in their place in the fruit bowl now buzzing with fruit flies. "Hey, aren't you going to eat those bananas?" I asked, with a hint of sarcasm in my voice. He did not look up from the frying pan, "No....why would I eat rotten bananas when I can have bacon and eggs?!" I laughed, "yes, why?"

But the fast had ended and although there had been some great breakthroughs, we had sought the Lord and He had answered some prayers, Robby woke up the next morning still covered in bumps and still itching. We waited. We knew that it is after the fast that God continues to bless and answer prayer, so our faith was strong that somehow God would bring us the miracle we had been believed for.

About a week after that first fast I got an excited voice message from my uncle who lives in Louisiana. He told me that he had stopped at a country grocery store and noticed that there was a display of lotion next to the counter. The name of the product was "Miracle II" and the sign said it helped things like "Eczema" and other skin issues. He had bought a big jug of it and was going to send it to us, and he believed it could be the "miracle" we were looking for! Well, you can imagine our praise as we waited for the miracle product to arrive! By this time Robby could not put ANY lotion on his skin, he couldn't use even the mildest of products, and as a result his skin was dry, brittle and he shed all over the place!

We thanked God for this answer to prayer! When Robby put a tiny bit on an infected area of his arm and there was no pain, no burning---we ALL praised God for this incredible miracle and for the next 10 years this "Miracle II" lotion was the only thing Robby ever put on his skin. It helped him dramatically, but it did not heal him.

Another year passed. We fasted throughout it, listening to the still, and quiet voice of God, seeking His direction in EVERY decision, and fasting when we needed a breakthrough of some kind. There was ALWAYS an answer to prayer—sometimes not exactly as we thought it would be answered, but we ALWAYS heard from God when we fasted.

THE PROMISE

The prophetic word that had been spoken over Robby was held tightly within my heart as a confirmation that there WOULD be an end to Robby's "suffering". He was only 14-years-old at the time of this prophesy, so our imaginations ran wild as to what it meant! We began sharing it with our family, most of whom, up to that point had never spoken much about God, or Christ, or church. Robby was our family's first born grandson and great-grandson- he was already highly favored by those who knew and loved him, so now having this new fire inside his belly was irresistible!

The suffering continued. In fact, the skin issues got steadily worse and worse, and I found myself many nights more than just *angry* at God. I was more than angry. There was an anointing on this young man, he was called to greatness, so how long did God expect him to suffer, me to suffer, his family to suffer as we watched him daily writhe in pain? This rash—this modern-day leprosy was all-controlling. It controlled where we went (beach? No sun for Robby) (out to eat? Most foods made him break out worse) (Movie? The constant scratching, itching and throat clearing made it impossible to sit quietly for any length of time). In and out of homeopathic doctor's offices, in and out of light treatments, colonics....vitamins, home remedies.....and I clung to the prophesy.

"You are going to be like and unto a Joseph in your family." What did that mean? I began to study the story of Joseph in the Bible. Certainly Joseph was the favored son of his father Jacob. Like Robby. Certainly Joseph suffered. He was thrown into a pit and left for dead by his jealous brothers because there was an anointing on his life! Then, thrown into prison after being falsely accused. Joseph suffered. But even in his suffering the hand of God remained strong in Joseph's life. Even in his prison he ministered and used his gift to help others....the parallels were undeniable. Robby's suffering seemed to be the affliction that he carried on his skin. Robby's ministry started at home, with us, his family. It was HIS passion for the Lord that motivated us to go to church. It was watching *him* worship the Lord that caused us, his parents, to begin to understand what a true relationship with Christ meant. And it was because of Robby that I watched my Mom walk down to an altar for the first time in my life. And then my grandmother, Mamaw—not only come

to really KNOW the Lord, but to get miraculously healed and have a vision of Christ in Heaven seated on the throne. Like Joseph, Robby brought our family out of a spiritual famine and into the abundance of God's love!

Robby's issues with his skin and the low self-esteem something like this can cause meant that he was "set apart" from the world in many ways. He was very social, his spirit was bigger than life, but his skin condition coupled with his desire to know more about the Lord caused him to spend lots of time alone, reading his Bible or praying. He made some amazing friends at his youth group. He wanted to be at the church every minute the doors were opened! Even though we lived an hour away, every Wednesday night either his father, Bobby would drive him, or my Mom would take him to make sure he was where he wanted to be. Ryan was just 5-years-old, the mid-week service was 'too much' for him, so he and I stayed home, but Robby grew in the Lord.

His compassion for young people was apparent, and we knew he was ministering to youth his age who were going through struggles—either with their parents, drugs, boyfriends, school or whatever, Robby listened and prayed with them. He had a gentle, soft spoken spirit and it attracted people of all ages to him! During this time he fasted on his own; we would often see him at the dinner table, carefully choosing to eat only the vegetables and we knew that he was fasting for something. It was a blessing to watch him grow in the Lord.

The years passed....we saw miracle after miracle happen for our family! Each year as we started the 21-Day fast our hearts were ready and open for the healing that was surely to come! I am sure that I have experienced a small inkling of the grief that Jacob suffered believing that his son Joseph was dead. Watching your child suffer from a disease that you are powerless to help him with is beyond comprehension. I truly do not know exactly how Robby felt or if he ever got mad at God (like I did). Sometimes when he would be down on the floor, hunched over scratching his legs, arms, neck, hands uncontrollably, Bobby and I would stand above him praying silently, trying not to let him see us cry. If we stayed too long the itching would intensify and crying, he would beg us to leave the room. My heart was torn as all I wanted to do was grab him up and hug him, but more than anything I could not bear to walk away. Bobby would tell him over and over, "If I could trade places with you, Robby, I would," and I would hear the words and guiltily think to myself, "I'm not so sure I could do that."

After a few moments we would hear him rise to his feet, he would breathe in a deep, deep breath and exhale loudly as if to say, "It's done." He suffered.

We fasted each year and saw many miracles come to pass, but still no healing for Robby. What do you do when you fast and still God does not answer? You fast some more! You believe bigger! You STAND on God's Word, you never, ever let go of the promise. I read about and felt I intimately knew every person who had received healing in the Bible. The woman with the issue of blood, the 10 lepers, Naaman who came up out of the river completely healed of leprosy, the blind man....even Lazarus who had risen from the dead! All I was asking was for my son to be healed.

The Sunday night altars were filled with dancing and worship, we loved, we laughed, and we watched our boys grow. We waited. We waited for what the prophet had promised us...." But brother, **at the end of that suffering,** you're going to be the catalyst that saves your family." There would be an end to the suffering. Months passed. Years passed. He graduated from high school—and now what career path would he choose?

I'll never forget the morning he came running up to me after a Wednesday night service. "Mom! There's some guys from church who have overcome drug addictions and God is calling them to open a new ministry that will help teenage boys get free of addictions! They want ME to be a part of it and help them open it! " He was bouncing around the kitchen as was typical for him (well, surely he gets this 'honest' as they say!) and could barely contain his excitement. I immediately began to question him about all the details, listening wide-eyed because I KNEW the time was coming when he would be walking into his anointing and as the man of God promised, there would be an end to his suffering.

THE THORN IN THE FLESH

He went on to tell me that these young men had found an abandoned Christmas tree farm just a few miles north of our church in Gainesville, and the land was beautiful, full of overgrown Christmas trees and 55-acres of God's country! The owners of the farm had given them permission to start the program that would eventually be called, "3-Dimensional Life" (3-D). Their plan was to open the ministry in October, work to trim and prune enough of the trees to sell during the Christmas season and use the profits to help support bringing the boys there in January. It seemed like God had opened an amazing door that excited Robby. Then he told me "the news". There was an abandoned school bus on the property that they were going to clean out, put in bunk beds and live there while working on the property. I tried desperately to hide my immediate fear of what would happen to Robby in a humid bus in the hot sun, the grass (which he was allergic to), the weeds- all the reasons why he would never be able to live in an abandoned bus like other young boys who didn't have this plague, this leprosy, this THORN IN THEIR FLESH that wouldn't go away. (2 Corinthians 12:7) I was not about to immediately dispel his dream, but I began to diligently pray, "Lord, PLEASE do not make this happen. Either heal him now or stop this from happening." The plans continued.

This new ministry was going to be amazing! The young men who were opening it had experienced many addictions and recovery programs, but none that were geared to *boys*. Both had graduated from a Christian recovery program called "No Longer Bound" (for men ages 21 and up) and I knew very well from the testimonies and evidence I had witnessed at church that God was about to do some amazing things in our son's life! *"At the end of the suffering...."* The words echoed in my mind and I clung to them daily.

Bobby and I were invited to go out and look at the land, and it was absolutely fabulous! It definitely showed the tell-tale signs of neglect, the weeds grew up around the front gate, which hung loosely on its hinges. The dirt road was full of pot holes and cracks—muddy even in the warm sunny day—and the little shack that served as the "retail shop" had holes and big cracks in the wood, and was desperately in need of a paint job, BUT--- the vision was there, the dream was big, and God was in it! The trees! Oh my, the trees! There were acres and acres of them....fields of this type and that, ALL overgrown and full of weeds—there were a few fields that had trees that 'might work' in size, but overall, well, I was reminded of "Charlie Brown's Christmas" and the sad little tree that he proudly produced!

We agreed that we would spend the weekends helping the small crew fix the place up to be ready for selling Christmas trees on the Friday after Thanksgiving—nothing short of a miracle! We had 5 boys, 4 sets of parents and a few friends who were supposed to transform this wild overgrown garden into a Christmas wonderland!

A few days before they were to move onto the property (and believe me I was consistently asking God HOW this was going to work) Robby came home again with some "over the top" exciting news. The owners of the property had been awakened the night before by a dream. They dreamed that the property was full of beautifully trimmed Christmas trees, full of life again, full of laughter, full of God. They had retired after owning the property for many years, and had moved to Florida to live out their days, but had been unable to sell it to a single owner and had refused many offers from investors who wanted to transform it into a subdivision, cutting down all the trees in the process. On the land they had built a beautiful log cabin type home, and in their dream they saw it full of the same laughter, the same love that they had experienced for so many years. It was the boys who were in recovery that were sitting next to the stone fireplace in their dream. They called the next morning and told the boys that they would be allowed to live on the property rent-free for 1 year, and then based on the production of the trees and other income generated from what the land produced, they could do a purchase of the entire property with no interest. All they really wanted was for someone to love the land as much as they had. The 5 boys immediately moved into the beautiful log home. I rested peacefully that night, knowing that God HAD answered a mother's prayer.

3-Dimensional Life is in its 14th year! So many lives changed because Robby and these young men stepped out in faith and were obedient to God. He learned so much there! We were a part of the family recovery program, we watched street-smart, angry, addicted boys metamorphosis into healthy, joyful young men under the leadership of this incredible ministry! We were a part of the healing of families, helping break generational curses of alcohol and drug abuse, not just off of these boys, but off of their fathers, their mothers, their sisters, their brothers. It was not easy. But it was worth it.

Another amazing testimony happened the year after 3-D was opened. The incredible testimonies and healing and release of addiction that happened regularly on that property was breathtaking! After the Christmas season was "over" and all the Christmas trees sold and everyone settling down to spend the holidays with their families, we set off for Louisiana which was our tradition to spend time with my Mom and family. While there, we got the impression that our nephew Beaux was involved in some drug activity; by this time we were aware of the signs and how to detect this type of abuse. He did his best to hide it, but on the ride home we all discussed that he was definitely involved in some serious addictions and agreed to pray that he would be miraculously delivered from them and come to know the Lord.

As the days prior to the fast began, as was our tradition we sat down and listed the prayer requests that we were fasting for, and as always "Robby's healing" was the top of the list. But that year, 2nd on the list was for Beaux. The fast began and our family prayed together, took communion together, and sought God in our own way. We set aside the "things of the world" and really took the time to go after God and to seek His direction.

The Monday after the fast was over I got a phone call from my brother, Buddy. He and Beaux were on their way to Atlanta from Louisiana. He told me that Beaux had been arrested for drug possession and the only way that he could keep Beaux out of jail was if he could get him into a drug rehab. Buddy was crying as he spoke and begged me to allow

Beaux to come to Atlanta (what could I say? They were on their way!) and help him get Beaux into the 3-D program. I hung up the phone and told Bobby what had happened. We were blown away that God was going to use us to answer our fasting prayer and certainly never expected it to happen so quickly!

It was not an easy time for our family. Helping someone beat and fight addiction is never easy. But by God's grace Beaux did end up getting registered into the program, he did get gloriously saved and Baptized and lived with us until he got his GED and some good job experience. Since this is the chapter of "Robby's Story" I will say that had Robby not been a part of Beaux's recovery process I don't believe it would ever have happened; it was Robby's sensitivity and the role model that he represented that propelled Beaux's healing.

WHAT ABOUT UNANSWERED PRAYER?

What do you do when your number one prayer request never seems to be answered? You **Fast** *again*. You **stand** on God's word. Many times I would cling to the story in the Bible where the widow continues to take her case before the unjust judge. It is found in Luke 18—" *And he (Jesus) spake a parable unto them to this end, that men ought always to pray, and not to faint."* Jesus uses this parable to explain to the disciples (and to us!) that we must continuously take our prayers to the Lord until He answers them. I read this story over and over and over; it gave me strength to Fast one more time, to pray one more time for Robby's healing.

Sometimes I would wonder if, like Paul, this disease for some reason was to be "Robby's thorn" in his flesh. The Bible never makes it clear exactly what Paul's "thorn" was, but it was obvious that Paul was doing God's work, was obedient to God, so why must he suffer?

"Paul speaks of a 'thorn in the flesh' in 2 Corinthians 12:7. He calls it 'a messenger of Satan' that had a purpose of "torment." Many explanations have been put forward, but whether Paul is referring to a physical, spiritual, or emotional affliction—or something else entirely—has never been answered with satisfaction. Since he was not talking of a literal thorn, he must have been speaking metaphorically. Some of the more popular theories of the thorn's interpretation include temptation, a chronic eye problem, malaria, migraines, epilepsy, and a speech disability. Some even say that the thorn refers to a person, such as Alexander the coppersmith, who did Paul 'a great deal of harm' (2 Timothy 4:14). No one can say for sure what Paul's thorn in the flesh was, but it was a source of real pain in the apostle's life." (http://www.gotquestions.org/Paul-thorn-flesh.html)

Some commentaries say that the purpose of this thorn was to keep Paul humble. To keep him from feeling "haughty" or prideful about what God had called him to do. I contemplated on this a lot. Was this disease going to be used by God for a purpose that we could not comprehend? And if so, would it be that God expected Robby to live with it for the rest of his life? I could not conceive of that thought, and beyond that I KNEW that Robby was never prideful, never wanted to be the center of attention, and in fact, felt that this disease kept him from walking strong into his destiny and the calling that God had put on his life. It caused him to fall into depression and even experience "self-hate" and lack of self-worth.

One of the lessons that can also be learned from this is that Paul would always claim that "God's grace was sufficient" for him to accept this thorn and continue to do the will of God and do all that God had assigned him to do. (2 Corinthians 12:9) Paul wrote much of the New Testament. It was obvious that God's Hand was on him and yet—and yet, God allowed this pain and suffering and affliction to remain with Paul his entire life. As a mom, I could not believe this was the path that was intended for Robby. I held onto the belief that Robby would be healed.

So many fasts....so many miracles. The miracle of Robby's healing.

THE FAST OF 2007.

It was in 2006 that Robby found a program that excited him. It is called "Master's Commission" and it's a "place to **LIVE**, truly live out the life God has called you to and to become a true **DISCIPLE** of Christ." (http://www.mastersusa.com/) It was a 3 year intense program which helped those who are called by the Lord to grow in intimacy with the Lord and pursue the dreams that God has put inside them. Robby was 21 years old at the time. We encouraged him to go through the Master's program and continue to grow in the Lord. His self-confidence was not where it needed to be in order for him to walk in the greatness that God had for him. We knew that there was some things God needed to do in him and through him.

Robby moved into an apartment with several other roommates and began to pursue the Master's commission program with all his heart, just as he had done everything else in his life. It was difficult for me as a Mom to have him move out of our house. After starting 3-D and spending 2 years there, the stress on his body was taking a huge toll. He was outside in the hot sun much of the time, it was difficult for him to eat the way he needed to eat in order to keep his skin issues at bay, so he spent much of his time in such pain that it was difficult to continue living on this beautiful property that God had provided for them. He had moved back home and I had been able to help him get his skin back under some control, and the environment at home was a healthier one than anywhere else. But, he was 21 years old and it was time for God's prophesy to be fulfilled.

I did my best not to worry that his skin issues would hinder his success, but I had seen it happen before and I will have to admit by 2006 I had grown very weary. Fast after fast, year after year, prayer after prayer. And Robby itched. I was not only weary, but I had begun experiencing some health challenges as well. I was going through some hormonal changes, depression, and anxiety. The high pressure business that we owned, coupled with some serious attacks from the enemy outside of our immediate family, and dealing with Robby's health issues were enough to knock any strong woman to her knees, and I was no exception. I had been having panic and anxiety attacks that had caused me to rarely leave my home except to go to church. I was gaining weight, felt miserable, had digestive issues and I had dealt with insomnia most of my life. 2006 had been a difficult year and I was eagerly awaiting the beginning of 2007 and the fast!

DURING the fast of 2007 nothing out of the ordinary happened. After fasting for so many years we knew that many times the answers to prayer, the miracles, come after the fast is long over and we have forgotten about it. But how can you fast for the same thing over and over and over again and still no real answers? It is easy to allow doubt and fear to set in, and for some reason after this fast I lost some traction in the "faith department." My depression worsened and my faith was truly at an all-time low.

By February the spiral was real and I was sinking into my own world, completely shutting out everyone and everything. The ONLY thing that I did was go to church every Wednesday night and every Sunday. My panic attacks started on Friday in anticipation of getting dressed to go to church on Sunday. All I could think about was going to bed at night, and when I went to bed I could not sleep. When the alarm rang I didn't want to get up. It was an endless cycle. My husband Bobby insisted that I do something, and encouraged me to go to a women-only fitness center in hopes that exercise and getting out of the house would help me. I agreed because I was completely miserable with my weight and hated myself. I began working out there 2-4 times per week during the day when few ladies were there.

I want to remind you that during this time I WAS A CHRISTIAN. I was serving in our church ministry, I was active in our church. I prayed, I read my Bible. I fasted. And yet, in spite of all that I was dealing with depression and sickness. What is wrong with that picture?

March 31, 2007. I was lying in bed struggling as always to sleep and found myself thinking about all we had been through with Robby. I will have to openly admit that I was definitely mad at God and I could not sleep. I got up, exhausted, went upstairs and began writing a letter to God. On top of the other issues I was dealing with I had severe carpal tunnel pain in both my hands and arms and typing the letter was extremely difficult. I know typing the letter was a pouring out of my spirit that had to be done, because somehow I was able to put down on paper exactly how I had been feeling. I told God in my letter that I just didn't trust Him anymore. I told Him that I was so hurt and mad that He had chosen not to heal Robby, and I wrote all the reasons that He SHOULD heal Robby. I reminded Him of His promises and told Him that I was disappointed in Him that He would lie to me. It was real and God already knew what I was thinking anyway, so I was not fearful that He would be angry at me. I wrote that in spite of all these things I would continue to love Him. In spite of all these things I was willing to forgive Him, and I was willing to continue serving Him. I told Him that I would NEVER allow myself to believe that Robby was going to be healed, and that I would NEVER pray that prayer again. I felt much better and very relieved after writing the letter. I cried the entire time, read it again to make sure that I hadn't left anything out, printed it, and then went back to bed. By now it was early in the morning hours and I slept more soundly than I had in a long time.

The next day was a Monday and Robby typically came home on Mondays and brought 2 or 3 other boys in the Master's Commission with him. They would do their laundry, eat a ton of food out of the fridge, and hang out for a few hours. I was completely exhausted from lack of sleep, but did my best not to let Robby see it. We were standing in the kitchen, rummaging through the fridge for leftovers, and I was standing at the stove about to cook some eggs when Robby came up behind me, excited. "Mom!", he said with great enthusiasm, "Something amazing happened last night and God told me He was going to heal me by the end of this year!" When he said it he put his hand on top of mine. I looked down at his precious hand. It was covered in sores. It was flaking and peeling and bloody streaks ran across it. It looked like the hand of an 80-year-old man who had been in the sun and worked hard labor his whole life. My heart stopped momentarily. I did not look up at Robby's face. Without emotion I managed to say, "That's great Robby."

I walked away from the stove to the fridge so that he would not see the tears that were welling up in my eyes. My thoughts were in chaos! The NERVE of God to play this game with my emotions. The NERVE of God to open up these emotions and to LIE to Robby. In the past I had always been Robby's biggest cheerleader about this. I was constantly assuring him, encouraging him, reminding him of God's promise. I had many visions of Robby's skin being like that of Naaman when he emerged from the muddy Jordan. But I had completely stopped believing. Robby followed me to the fridge, grabbed me by my shoulders and spun me around. "MOM! Did you hear what I said? God told me He is going to heal me by the end of the year!" I managed to smile broadly and wipe away the tears quickly. He mistook the tears for tears of joy and my acting talents were stretched as I celebrated this news with him. It was all I could do not to burst into tears and I could not wait for them to leave so I could scream and cry. We ate some lunch, did some laundry and caught up, but my heart was not in the conversation. I just wanted to roll up in a ball and die.

When they finally left I went upstairs to my desk and laid my head down on it and began to sob uncontrollably. I pounded my fist on my desk and questioned God. Why? Why would He be so cruel?

I was startled by my office phone ringing and looked at the caller ID, knowing that whomever it was would have to wait, I was in no mood to talk to customers or clients. But, I saw that it was the cable company calling who I had been trying to reach for several days, so I was forced to pick it up. The woman's voice on the other end of the line initially confused me. I looked back at the caller ID and realized that it was only 1 number off from the cable company's number, and this was not who I thought it was. The woman continued to talk, "This is Jan—I met you at the workout facility a few weeks ago." Oh God I thought, not now! I do not have time or energy to talk to this woman nor do I need a new friend. I remembered vaguely giving her my number one afternoon when she asked for it, knowing it was unlikely that I would ever answer the phone when she called.

"Hi Jan, listen, I am working right now, and I really don't have time to talk—"

"I understand," she insisted, "But remember when you were talking about your son Robby and his skin disease?"

My heart stopped again. "Yes."

"Well, I wanted to tell you that I have a good friend whose son had skin issues just like Robby, but she was able to get it completely cleared up. And I thought you might want to speak with her."

What? Are you serious, God?

"Okay, sure, but I only have a moment." I struggled to keep control of my emotions.

"Great. I have her on hold, her name is Faith and you are going to love meeting her."

My head and thoughts were spinning out of control. It was like a strange dream and I was watching myself listen to this woman share her story about her son. It was as if I was hearing Robby's story…"covered with a rash at birth" "the doctors couldn't do anything for us" "we did everything possible nutritionally after that" "nothing worked" "we prayed." The only difference was that Faith's son was still very young (I don't remember how old he was) when she found the solution for him. And the solution came in the form of "powder in a can." She explained that there was this nutritional product that she had found and after a very short time of him taking it he quit itching, and then the wounds healed and now, today he was symptom free of all that had plagued him.

Jan asked me if I was interested in hearing more. Robby's words rang in my ears, "God told me He was going to heal me by the end of the year." I thought it intensely ironic that when I no longer had FAITH, God sent a sweet woman named Faith to share this hope with me! He sent me "Faith".

"Yes, I need to know more." I collapsed on my desk in utter exhaustion. After an hour I called Robby and told him about the phone call. Then I told him what had happened the night before and about my letter to God. I know he was crying silent tears on the other end of the phone. We had been through such a journey together, was this how God was going to heal him?

He began taking this powerful nutritional product on April 3, 2007. 2 weeks later it was Spring Break for Master's Commission so he was staying at home, and by now he had been faithfully taking the product. He came up the basement stairs that morning as I was cooking breakfast. I had gotten into a habit of looking at his arms each morning. If they were raw and bleeding I could tell that he had not had a good night. It meant he had clawed and scratched and open wounds and dried blood were indicators. I instinctively surveyed his arms. He looked at me with such intensity. He spoke softly, "Mom, I was lying in bed last night and I just started to cry. It was the first time that I have ever felt comfortable in my own skin."

His health improved dramatically over the course of the next few months. He scratched less and less at night giving the wounds time to heal. His allergies improved. The tickle in his throat cleared up and the chronic cough he had had for so many years went away. He was able to do things he had never done before. We could hug him and touch him without him flinching away in pain. It was nothing less than miraculous.

But it wasn't a miracle just for Robby. Our entire family began taking this nutritional product and the health of all of us changed dramatically. Within 2 weeks I had lost 10 pounds! I had no more symptoms of the carpal tunnel pain, I was sleeping through the night and my hormones seemed to be in a better balance. God had used this nutrition to heal our bodies. Looking back, no one could possibly have known the impact that would have on our futures and on the lives of hundreds of other people who I would touch as a wellness coach.

There are a couple of ways that I could go with this chapter at this point. There is much, much more to Robby's story. The prophetic word that was spoken over him has come into fruition many times over, and even now, at the WRITING of this book Robby is about to step into yet another level of his ministry that will stretch him and his family more than ever before. I do feel there is a time and a place to share more about Robby's journey, but let me share this—he met an amazing woman named Katrina at the Master's Commission. They married in August of 2009 and have 3 beautiful HEALTHY children. As of today Shalom is 4, Mikha'el is 2, and Maryrose will be 1-year-old in less than a month. We are blessed. God is about to send them as a family on a 10 week mission trip and when they return they will be used by God to train other missionary families. Robby just turned 30. What a huge blessing.

THE FAST OF 2008

We call this fast our "Celebration and Thanksgiving Fast". 2007 had been an incredible year of miracle after miracle in so many ways for our family, and although Robby was not completely healed, the change in the quality of his life was dramatic and we knew once again that God had His hand on our family. Robby and I both celebrated and gave thanks to God with a 40 Day Fast. During this time we drank only water and took the nutritional supplement that God had provided for us and we felt amazing! We did not ask God for anything during that fast, we just worshipped Him and gave thanks for answering our prayers for Robby.

It was during that 40 day fast that God called me into my purpose and ministry. He called me to be a healer, He anointed my hands to heal and showed me things about nutrition to help others heal. I was able to lay hands on people and they were instantly healed, and through Him many miracles happened even DURING that fast.

I have been mightily blessed to have helped families with all kinds of diseases using this nutritional product and the knowledge that God has given me, and over the past few years have completely changed what I eat and drink in order to keep my body healthy in a world surrounded by disease and death.

As a result of changing the way I have been eating, avoiding processed foods and building my immune system, I am walking in the health that the Bible promises us. Since April of 2007 I have not had a cold, a sniffle, a flu or stomach virus. I haven't even had a headache. I am 55 years old as of the writing of this book and I have no pain in my body. I sleep well, have tons of energy. I am no longer depressed. I no longer have panic and anxiety attacks. God has healed my body through nutrition.

CONCLUSION

Throughout this book I talked about living a lifestyle of fasting. I talked about how God has called the church to stand apart from and eat differently than the world. I believe that this message is going to resonate with a few who read it. Many who read this will say it is "too hard." It certainly isn't easy. I will admit that. At least, it isn't easy at first. Today, more than 5 years later it is a lifestyle that I would not change if I could. I occasionally eat a dessert. Every once in a while I eat a piece of pizza. But when I do it is a calculated risk, not just because everyone else is doing it.

It was not until this year, this Fast that God showed me that the lifestyle that our family has adopted is one that will save us from the diseases that the rest of the world will experience. He has chosen me to carry this message to the church, to His people so that they will have the energy and health they need to carry their cross, to share the good news of His love and of His healing power. Have I seen instantaneous healing miracles? I have! Many, many miracles as I personally laid hands on people—as I watched in services at many churches across the country and suddenly pain goes away, diseases leave their bodies as the hand of God touches them! God is definitely in the healing and miracle business.

But there are too many Christians in the altars of our churches and because of lifestyle choices they have made their bodies are broken and diseased. They are praying to God to heal their bodies and yet they are putting in this contaminated fuel that breaks it down even more. We all know too well that if we put the wrong fuel into the tanks of our vehicles, over time the car will not perform as well as it should, and eventually it will break completely down. Most people are willing to take better care of their cars, boats, motorcycles, homes, and even computers than they are of the temple that God has given them—their bodies! We complain of sickness and yet we do not do what the experts tell us to do. Sadly, too many of us are running to our doctors to save us from disease, when in fact, all they can do is prescribe medicines with side-effects that will at some point catch up with us.

This is not an easy message to carry. Trust me, for many months I have begged God to give me an easier message. I have asked Him to take away this burden that I have for the sick. I know there will be people who read this who will think that I do not have faith in a God who heals. Believe me, more than anyone I KNOW that God has and does heal instantly and miraculously. But I also know that there are too many good Christians who are dying needlessly because the enemy has deceived us. The enemy wants nothing more than for Christians to be as sick as the world, as poor as the world. The Bible tells us that Christ came so that we would have an abundant life! An *abundant* life! (John 10:10) That same verse says that our enemy comes to steal, kill and destroy. I am afraid that as Christians we have come to accept headaches, migraines, allergies, ADD, diabetes, high blood pressure, the flu, arthritis, depression as inevitable. We have given in to the lies of the enemy. I just recently read that they have just passed a law that doctors can prescribe anti-depressants to children as young as 6-years-old! This is a tragedy.

If we would be willing to stand out from the crowd as Daniel did, and say, "I will not eat from the King's table. It isn't good for me and it isn't healthy for me and I desire to live in the fullness of health that God has for me" there would be many, many more Christians on the mission field of our cities and churches who have the energy and money to take care of the widows and orphans as God has commanded us to do! (James 1:27) Daniel was a young man. He was given an open door to eat anything he wanted from the King's table, and you better believe it smelled and tasted good. He was a man with fleshly desires, just like you and me. It was not easy for him to say "no" to the delicacies of the world. There are many times that I go to a party and the food looks and smells so delicious. I am grateful to God that He has given me the strength to say "no" just as Daniel did. It didn't happen overnight for me. I still am not perfect. Until this year I ate the way I did only because it helped me keep my weight under control and kept me healthy. When God gave me the revelation during this fast that as Christians we are CALLED to live a lifestyle of fasting, I realized that He also commissioned me to be the EXAMPLE so that others could follow. When God showed me that my body is capable of stopping a disease such as cancer only because I had lived a lifestyle of eating the right things, it was a confirmation that we do not have to live with the diseases that we accept as "normal" and that I am to share this message in this book and as I am asked to speak in churches and women's groups across the country. (See my blog, "The Diagnosis Everyone Wants to Hear" TraceeRandall.com)

The message of salvation is so important. The message of grace, the message that Christ came and died on the cross and resurrected and because of that we are given eternal life—this message is so important. But if the soldiers are sick who is going into the battlefield? This lifestyle of fasting will equip us to have the energy and good health AND GOOD TESTIMONY to do what God has called us to do.

This year as I have been invited to speak for different groups and when the food is served there is always this embarrassment that they know they are not serving the "right foods" but it is so socially acceptable and EXPECTED to serve cake and ice-cream that the hostess or serving committee feel they haven't done their job if they didn't serve it! They look at me sheepishly as I politely refuse the delicacy, and now become embarrassed by that. All eyes are on me as I pass the cake on to the next person, and then eyes averted away as they guiltily pile it on their plate. I laugh to myself thinking the situation is much like a pastor who has finished preaching and then the alcohol is brought out—well, almost the same! People run out the back door to hide their cigarettes from the pastor, and put their wine in paper cups hoping no one else will know, but pass the cake openly—even when there is every evidence out there that sugar is a drug as harmful as cocaine is on the brain—only because the world has tricked us into believing it is okay. I recently had a few ladies over to my home and served a huge table of fresh fruits, veggies, healthy dips and sauces and everyone ate it like it was candy. As the conversation (as it always does) went to weight they wanted to lose and they munched on HEALTHY delicious snacks that would help them achieve that goal.

I often find myself smiling inwardly when I am in a room of people who have just been served a "King's meal" and most of the conversation turns to the aches and pains, diseases, health issues that they and their children have been dealing with—as they cram their mouths full of the very poison that is at the root of the problem. I am reminded of the story of the "blind leading the blind" as they give advice to each other with no idea of how to stop this vicious cycle of ill health they have been on! I smile inwardly, but truthfully it makes my stomach turn that they are so deceived. It makes me hurt for the children. Our children, our legacy.

God has given me great creative ideas during this year's fast. He is showing me that I am going to teach the Christians of the world how to make these changes, and it starts with a fast. It starts with denying your body of foods that are not serving you well, denying your flesh of foods for a period of time in order to seek the Lord. This book is just the beginning of the message that God has given me. Much like Dave Ramsey has turned the Christian world upside down (in a good way) to help them with their finances, I have been called to create programs that churches and Christians can follow that will take them to a new level of health! At the release of this book these programs are still being formed, and God is still bringing the right people into my path who will help me fulfill this God-given dream.

If you are reading this, there are many ministries and programs that you support or would like to support. Perhaps God has put a vision in your heart to make a difference in the world. Perhaps you have been called onto the mission field or are a trainer of missionaries. Maybe you are a pastor or you lead a women's Bible study. Maybe you are a children's pastor or work in children's church. Whatever God has called YOU to do, the only way to do it is to be healthy, full of energy and not distracted by pain and sickness! The only way to show people the power of God's healing is to be healthy yourself. Trust me, people are laughing at us when we preach to them that our God heals and the next week we are at the doctor's office with a heart condition or even allergies! They laugh at us and we lose our integrity and our witness and our testimony. We are seen as weak and shallow instead of strong and powerful!

The enemy is laughing at us too. He has most of us right where he wants us. Spending time at the doctor's offices instead of ministering to the homeless. He has our wallets right in his grip too. We are spending our money paying for medications and hospitals rather than feeding the hungry and clothing the poor. Tithes are down in the churches, offerings are down, the healthcare system is completely upside down, so this is a message that you better listen to. I am reminded about the story of the man who was sent to hell and begged to leave to go warn his brothers. (Luke 16:28) He was told that his brothers had plenty of warning just as he had, and was not allowed to go. Why is it we wait until we get the diagnosis to begin to make the changes? And even then we don't really know what to do.

Let's start with a fast. The "Daniel Fast" for 3 days. Eat only vegetables and fruits and drink water with lemon. Eat as much as you want and seek God to show you what your lifestyle of fasting should be. Ask Him for the strength to make the changes to live a lifestyle that is pleasing to Him. Ask Him to give you the resolve of Daniel as he stood before the King's table so many years ago, refusing to pollute his body with foods that were not good for him, and being obedient to the God that He worshipped and loved.

THERE'S PLENTY OF ROOM IN MIRACLE TERRITORY

Don't wait until the beginning of next year to start your fast. Do it now! Prepare for it and buy the foods that you will eat during the fast and prepare your place of worship and prayer. Set a date to start your fast and stick to it. Don't wait until there are no parties, or conferences or trips or distractions—that day never comes. Just set a date and stick to it. I like to start my fasts on a Sunday. Sundays are set aside to rest and to go to church and worship the Lord. What better day to take it to the next level and worship Him in fasting? If you have never fasted before don't start with a full fast—do the "Daniel Fast" for 3 days and seek the Lord with all your heart. Set aside some time to read the Bible (maybe read the book of Daniel) and set some time aside to LISTEN for the voice of God to speak to you. Ask Him to show you YOUR destiny. Each of us was born with a purpose, so are YOU! A fast will help you discern what God has for you and fulfill the prophecy that God has spoken over YOUR life!

Expect miracles. The Bible tells us that God is ready to give us the desires of our hearts, IF we will delight in Him! *"Take delight in the LORD, and he will give you the desires of your heart." (Psalm 37:4).* What ARE the desires of your heart? Don't know? You will be amazed when you ask Him!

This year has been one of the most powerful of my life so far, and it is only half over! I love walking in miracle territory and in alignment with God's plan for my life. There's plenty of room in miracle territory! Come join me!

LET'S BEGIN—YOUR WORKBOOK & FASTING JOURNAL

WHAT ARE YOU FASTING FOR?

Let's **attach our prayers with our FAST**—By attaching your prayers to the FAST it will help you stay on track! It's easy to forget WHY you are FASTing when there is so much food around us, everywhere we go! What are the desires of your heart? There are 8 areas of your life-- take a look at each area and write what you would like to improve or change? Write specific prayer requests or goals regarding each of the 8 areas of your life. Keeping your life in balance will help you achieve your goals! JOURNALING while FASTing is so important as well! Take the time to really think about each area and write it down as you prepare to FAST. Write down what you would like to improve about each area of your life, and then make a poster for your kitchen, prayer room, bedroom, car—every area of your home so that you can always look at it and be reminded, this is WHY I committed to FASTing!

AREAS OF YOUR LIFE:

1. Spouse—Many times in our hustle and bustle we tend to take our spouse for granted. This year, 2015, as I FASTED I realized that I had definitely taken my incredible husband, Bobby for granted, so I began to

pray for God to change ME. Sometimes we focus on the negative characteristics of our spouse, which causes us to feel dissatisfied in our marriages and relationships. This was my prayer in 2015: "Lord, please show me how to love Bobby more. Please make me a better wife and help me love him more!" This year has been magical! Bobby and I have grown so much closer and we have had more fun together this year than we have in many years! What is your prayer?

_____
_____
_____
_____
_____
_____

2. Health/Body--Do you need healing in any area of your body? Jesus took the stripes on His back for our healing--His desire for us is that we should walk in good health (3 John 1:2 "Beloved, I wish above all things that thou mayest prosper and be in health, even as thy soul prospereth.")

Lord, help me to continue to make better food choices & continue fasting. Heal every part of my body that is not operating @ 100% the way you designed it to. Help me to lose weight & to keep it off in a healthy manner.

3. **Job/Business**

Many of us are living paycheck to paycheck and are struggling to survive. My question to you is this--how can we bless other people financially if we can't feed our own families? If you need help in your finances, it's time to "believe God" for a miracle! Ask God to give you creative ideas for a business or how to improve in your job so that your value goes up! Are there areas of your business or work areas that need improvement? As Christians we should always set the example of being the hardest worker in every situation—what areas would you like to change?

Lord, I do the work @ DFCS, please release the increase + the back pay. Please show me how to properly fund a conference. Please increase the registration + vendors + advertisements for NMD. Please show me how to increase sales for Lily of Bijjle Sales.

4. Home/Environment—God showed me this year that I needed to clean up some clutter in my home in order to have a place that allowed me to walk in the fullness He has for me. I realized that I had been 'holding on' to some physical things that were not necessary. What is it that you have been holding on to that need to be thrown away? Your physical environment is important! Are you taking care of your home, even if you are renting it? Set some goals in this area of your life!

Help me to declutter my life + reorganize. Give me my tile back to clean + the energy to do it. Help me to let go + to make room. I want to be better.

5. Relationships with Family/Friends—God cannot hear our prayers if there is unforgiveness and bitterness in our hearts. Who do you need to forgive? Do you need to forgive YOURSELF for some things in order to walk in the fullness God has for you? What about your relationship with your children? Ask God to show you how to improve this area of your life. What specific prayer requests do you have for your family and/or children?

Show me where + how to improve any relationships. — Amanda — Codei + protect Kids + AJ. Help Kechan to finish college + prepare to work + live in this evil world. Heal the relationship more w/ Kia + I. This her.

6. Fun/Recreation—God delights in our happiness! He created us to laugh and enjoy life. Sometimes as Christians we carry so many burdens and can be so serious that we are not spreading peace and joy to others. Make a decision to take some time to enjoy yourself this upcoming year! Ask God to show you what you LIKE to do—and create some time to do it. For me this year it was to spend more time writing and reading—and going to antique shops and just browsing. How can you add fun into your life?

Music makes me happy. Please make a way for me to record the songs I've written. Traveling. Please make a way for travel, relaxation + fun.

7. Mind/Spiritual—Are you connected to a good church? A church that is alive and exciting and sharing the Word of God? The Bible tells us that we should connect together as believers and lift each other up and pray for each other. Maybe there is a great Bible study group or small group that you can connect with that will help you in your Christian walk. Are you reading and listening to great, positive CD's or music? Remember what you listen to and focus on is so important. If you listen to 'talk radio' or even the news all the time it is easy to become negative and even depressed. Make sure you are feeding your mind with positive and uplifting information on a daily basis. Ask God to show you the right things to listen to!

8. Finances—This is different from your job/business. Setting long-term goals about your future is so important! Planning for college or retirement and making sure that you are not in debt or overspending is vital to your balance in life. As Christians we should be responsible in this area—ask God to connect you to the right people or program that can help you with your finances!

List more of your prayer requests here. I encourage you to BE SPECIFIC and be BOLD in your requests. Ask God to show you His direction and plan for your life:

$25,000 for NMD
958 S. Hairston for DGMI
- Money to do ALL Necessary work
- Great Bible Believers to help run the Ministry
- Increased sales for LWR + book sales
- AKITA - JOY, HAPPINESS, WALK in her CALLING Fully.

PRAISE HIM!

Now! It's time to PRAISE HIM for all that you have! It's time to count your blessings! The Bible tells us that we must be thankful in all things, our gratitude pleases God, AND we must take time every day to thank God for all He has given us.

(1 Thessalonians 5:16-18 "Rejoice always, pray without ceasing, give thanks in all circumstances; for this is the will of God in Christ Jesus for you.")

Many times we focus on what we don't have instead of what we DO HAVE. You will be so blessed when you make the decision to show gratitude and give thanks for everything you have!

Just recently God showed me powerfully how important it is to be GRATEFUL for what we have. It's easy to become complacent and want more than we have and it can cause us to live a life that is frustrating! Bobby and I had fallen into this pattern- focusing on the stack of bills that kept mounting up, the refrigerator breaking down the day after Thanksgiving and all our left-overs ruined, issues with the cars, with our business- it just seemed that these issues were mounting and Bobby especially was struggling to have peace—the enemy was causing discord between us and we were so frustrated.

One Friday afternoon we were across town running some errands when we stopped in at a Chic-Filet for a quick bite to eat. As we pulled up I noticed a man sitting on the concrete steps—it was so bitterly cold that day and he was sitting hunched over with a blue hood over his head. I couldn't see his face but I knew he must be cold. I commented on him to Bobby and we decided that he must be on a lunch break as there was a service truck parked directly behind him.

As we sat in the warmth of the restaurant, I noticed that the service truck had driven away and the man was still sitting there on the cold cement steps; he had not moved. Something came over me (the Holy Spirit) and I stood up and told Bobby I was going to see if he was okay. Miraculously, Bobby didn't stop me.

I walked and stood a couple of feet from him and said, "Excuse me, are you okay?" When he looked up I noticed the deepness of his eyes. He smiled and said, "Sure, I'm okay, but I am homeless." He said it matter-of-factly and it startled me. We began to talk and he shared that he had only been homeless for a year, and that he was looking for a job, but it was difficult. Just a year earlier he had a home, a wife, a son—but all had been stripped away by a bitter divorce that left him homeless. I don't know why I asked him the next question, but I am so glad that I did, "How does it feel to be homeless?"

His name was Yul- he was 33 years-old. He looked up at me again, and I heard him say, "Every day that I wake up I tell myself that I am blessed and highly favored." My heart melted. What an incredible testimony! Yul had a smile that originated straight from his heart, and in spite of his circumstances he smiled a lot, and he wasn't looking for a handout or pity.

The lesson that Bobby and I learned that day was priceless. We were ashamed of our recent whining to each other about what we DIDN'T have and were so grateful to God for what we HAVE. (Yes! We helped Yul—and what a testimony THAT was! Be sure and read my blog on my website titled "Yul-Tide Blessings" and find out what happened to and for Yul as a whole community came together to bless him!) But—more than we blessed Yul, HE blessed US! I will never forget that moment. I will always feel "blessed and highly favored" no matter my circumstances!

WHAT ARE YOU GRATEFUL FOR?

Make a list of at least 10 things that you are GRATEFUL for! (Philippians 4:8 "And now, dear brothers and sisters, one final thing. Fix your thoughts on what is true, and honorable, and right, and pure, and lovely, and admirable. Think about things that are excellent and worthy of praise.")

I am happy and grateful for:

1. To BE ALIVE
2. To be Mostly healthy
3. Beautiful Children + Sweet AJ
4. Able to pay Most of My bills
5. God allowed Me to live here
6. God granted My car wish
7. God Sustains my job
8. God has not turned His back on me
9. Someone cares for me.
10. Those who do love + Support me & the Ministry God has for me.

JOURNALING

BEFORE THE FAST BEGINS

As I shared earlier in the book, each year our church calls a corporate FAST that begins the first Sunday of the year and ends 21-days later. There is so much power when people come together as believers and FAST and believe God to 'show up' in their lives! I invite you to join us the first of each year as a FIRST FRUITS offering and corporate FAST—in 2016 God showed me to create an on-line FASTing group on Facebook where people can come together from around the world and learn more about FASTing and join us as we dedicate the first 21-days of each year to the Lord. If you would like to be a part of that group, please email me and in the subject write, "I Want to Join Your FASTing Group" and I will make sure that happens!

Last year, as I began preparing my mind, body and spirit to FAST the first 21-days of the year, I began doing what I do naturally, that is- JOURNAL. I have already given you a couple of excerpts from my journal, and what a blessing to be able to look back at what I wrote and again, be amazed at what God has done! It is important that you begin the journaling process now—as you meditate in the mornings and begin to seek God and ASK HIM to show you the desires of your heart, write down thoughts and questions. One of the things I want to encourage you to do is just WRITE without thinking about it too much. Commit to journaling each morning and/or each evening and you will be amazed at what God reveals to you EVEN BEFORE the FAST through this process. Remember, NO ONE else will read your journal—it's between YOU and God. If it doesn't come easy for you at first, that is okay! Just WRITE. Some days I don't feel inspired to write, but I start my journal like this:

"Date: 12/16/14 Thursday 10:45am I am so excited about this upcoming FAST. I can't wait to see what new things and new ideas God reveals to me. I am so tired of doing everything on my own......."

This might help you get started on the journaling process. Write as little or as much as you want, but WRITE. You will find that God will begin to speak to you even BEFORE the FAST begins! Begin to write down what you want God to help you with next year! What goals do you have? Begin writing them down here in this book in the area provided so that you will have a record of your thoughts and dreams and goals. Journaling will prepare your mind and spirit for this upcoming FAST!

DURING THE FAST

Journaling every day is very important during a FAST. One of the things I love about journaling is that it is a way to go back and LOOK at what God has done, long after the FAST is over, God is still working on our behalf! I encourage you to write something every single day—starting a few days before the FAST, and then each morning and each evening DURING the FAST. Use this area of the book to begin your journaling—I have provided scripture references to meditate upon each day, and of course I encourage you to seek God and find your OWN scripture that speaks to YOU as well.

Keeping an on-going journal throughout the year is so important. Writing is a lost art and it is a true shame. I believe that if you will be faithful to writing something every day for 21-days you will SEE the power in it and it will become an ongoing habit that will benefit you in many ways! The area for journaling is provided for you here in the back of this book, so be sure and be faithful to this part of the FASTing process!

FASTING JOURNAL 21-DAY FIRST FRUITS FAST

JOURNALING BEFORE THE FAST—Remember, if you would like to join us in our corporate 21-Day FASTing group, contact me and I will make you a part of it! Email me <u>Tracee@TraceeRandall.com</u>.

Use this area of the book to begin journaling BEFORE the FAST begins. I would suggest beginning around December 15th so that you have a good 2-3 weeks before the actual FAST begins (the 1st Sunday of the year). If you aren't familiar with journaling, don't worry—just WRITE something every day—even if it is a simple prayer request, and 'thank you' for a small miracle or a burden you need to release to God. You will find that the more you journal the more you will WANT to journal! Have fun with this!

December 15th:

_____
_____
_____
_____
_____
_____
_____
_____
_____
_____
_____

December 16th:

December 17th:

December 18th:

December 19th:

December 20th:

December 21st:

December 22nd:

December 23rd:

December 24th:

December 25th: Christmas Day!

December 26th:

December 27th:

December 28th:

December 29th:

December 30th:

December 30st:

December 31st:

The FASTest Way to God's Favor and Blessing

21-DAY FAST—BEGINS _____ *(First Sunday in Jan.)*
ENDS _____

January—FIRST DAY OF THE FAST—DAY 1- Isaiah 40:31—But those who wait on the Lord shall renew their strength; They shall mount up with wings like eagles, They shall run and not be weary, They shall walk and not faint. (NKJV)

Date: _____ **Day:** _____ **Time:** _____

_____
_____
_____
_____
_____
_____
_____
_____
_____
_____
_____
_____
_____

Day 2– Philippians 4:8 (NKJV) Meditate on These Things- Finally, brethren, whatever things are true, whatever things *are* noble, whatever things *are* just, whatever things *are* pure, whatever things *are* lovely, whatever things *are* of good report, if *there is* any virtue and if *there is* anything praiseworthy—meditate on these things.

Date: _____ **Day:** _____ **Time:** _____

_____
_____

___

Day 3– Psalm 37:1 (NIV) Do not fret because of those who are evil or be envious of those who do wrong.

Date: _____ **Day:** _____ **Time:** _____

___

Day 4– James 1:27 (NIV) Religion that God our Father accepts as pure and faultless is this: to look after orphans and widows in their distress and to keep oneself from being polluted by the world.

Date: _____ **Day:** _____ **Time:** _____

_____
_____
_____
_____
_____
_____
_____
_____
_____
_____
_____

Day 5-- **Romans 8:28 (NIV)** And we know that in all things God works for the good of those who love him, who[a] have been called according to his purpose.

Date: _____ **Day:** _____ **Time:** _____

_____
_____
_____
_____
_____
_____
_____
_____
_____
_____
_____
_____

Day 6-- **Matthew 18:19 (NIV)** "Again, truly I tell you that if two of you on earth agree about anything they ask for, it will be done for them by my Father in heaven."

Date: _____ **Day:** _____ **Time:** _____

_____
_____
_____

_____
_____
_____
_____
_____
_____
_____
_____
_____
_____

Day 7-- **Isaiah 25:1(NIV)** Lord, you are my God; I will exalt you and praise your name, for in perfect faithfulness you have done wonderful things, things planned long ago.

Date: _____ **Day:** _____ **Time:** _____

_____
_____
_____
_____
_____
_____
_____
_____
_____
_____
_____
_____

Day 8-- <u>Psalm 139:14</u> **(NIV)** I praise you because I am fearfully and wonderfully made; your works are wonderful, I know that full well.

Date: _____ **Day:** _____ **Time:** _____

_____
_____
_____

_____
_____
_____
_____
_____
_____
_____
_____

Day 9-- Psalm 27:1 (NIV) The Lord is my light and my salvation—whom shall I fear? The Lord is the stronghold of my life—of whom shall I be afraid?

Date: _____ **Day:** _____ **Time:** _____

_____
_____
_____
_____
_____
_____
_____
_____
_____
_____
_____
_____

Day 10-- Philippians 4:13 (NIV) I can do all this through Him who gives me strength.

Date: _____ **Day:** _____ **Time:** _____

_____
_____
_____
_____

_____
_____
_____
_____
_____
_____
_____
_____
_____

Day 11-- John 10:10 (NIV) The thief comes only to steal and kill and destroy; I have come that they may have life, and have it to the full. (Note:-- so many times we hear Christians quoting the first part of this verse—all about the enemy—let's focus on the 2nd part, Jesus has come so that we have LIFE and have it to the fullest—abundant life in every area of our lives! I love this promise!)

Date: _____ **Day:** _____ **Time:** _____

_____
_____
_____
_____
_____
_____
_____
_____
_____
_____
_____
_____
_____
_____

Day 12-- John 3:16 (NIV) For God so loved the world that he gave his one and only Son, that whoever believes in him shall not perish but have eternal life.

Date: _____ **Day:** _____ **Time:** _____

_____
_____
_____
_____

___

Day 13—Jeremiah 29:11 (NIV) For I know the plans[1] I have for you," declares the LORD, "plans to prosper[2] you and not to harm you, plans to give you hope and a future."

Date: _____ **Day:** _____ **Time:** _____

___

Day 14-- Hebrews 11:1 (NIV) Now faith is the substance of things hoped for, the evidence of things not seen.

Date: _____ **Day:** _____ **Time:** _____

___

_____
_____
_____
_____
_____
_____
_____
_____

Day 15-- 2 Timothy 1:7 (KJV) For God hath not given us the spirit of fear; but of power, and of love, and of a sound mind.

Date: _____ **Day:** _____ **Time:** _____

_____
_____
_____
_____
_____
_____
_____
_____
_____
_____
_____
_____
_____

Day 16-- 1 Corinthians 10:13 (NIV) No temptation has overtaken you except what is common to mankind. And God is faithful; he will not let you be tempted beyond what you can bear. But when you are tempted, he will also provide a way out so that you can endure it.

Date: _____ **Day:** _____ **Time:** _____

_____
_____
_____
_____

_____
_____
_____
_____
_____
_____
_____
_____

Day 17-- Proverbs 22:6 (NKJV) Train up a child in the way he should go, and when he is old he will not depart from it.

Date: _____ **Day:** _____ **Time:** _____

_____
_____
_____
_____
_____
_____
_____
_____
_____
_____
_____
_____
_____

Day 18-- Joshua 1:9 (NKJV) Have I not commanded you? Be strong and of good courage; do not be afraid, nor be dismayed, for the LORD YOUR GOD *is* with you wherever you go.

Date: _____ **Day:** _____ **Time:** _____

_____
_____
_____
_____
_____

Day 19-- James 5:16 (NIV) Therefore confess your sins to each other and pray for each other so that you may be healed. The prayer of a righteous person is powerful and effective.

Date: _____ **Day:** _____ **Time:** _____

Day 20-- Deuteronomy 31:6 (NIV) Be strong and courageous. Do not be afraid or terrified because of them, for the LORD YOUR GOD GOES WITH YOU; HE WILL NEVER LEAVE YOU NOR FORSAKE YOU.

Date: _____ **Day:** _____ **Time:** _____

The FASTest Way to God's Favor and Blessing

_____
_____
_____
_____
_____
_____
_____
_____
_____
_____

Day 21-- Deuteronomy 8:18 (NIV) But remember the Lord your God, for it is he who gives you the ability to produce wealth, and so confirms his covenant, which he swore to your ancestors, as it is today.

Date: _____ **Day:** _____ **Time:** _____

_____
_____
_____
_____
_____
_____
_____
_____
_____
_____
_____
_____
_____

TRACEE RANDALL — BIO

Success in business comes easily for **author, speaker,** and **entrepreneur** Tracee Randall, who has a knack for taking an average business from mediocrity to great success using her innate business sense and creativity. She and her husband, Bobby, have been business owners and entrepreneurs for more than 30 years. They have built several million-dollar corporations in the service and relocation industries.

Tracee is considered by many to be one of Georgia's foremost Wellness Transformation Coaches--she is recognized internationally as a speaker and is now an author in the best-selling book series titled "The Change--Insights to Empowerment." Her article "Saving Money by Staying Healthy" was featured nationally online during America Saves Week, and her signature coaching program, "50 Weeks and 50 New Habits", is transforming hundreds of lives physically, emotionally, financially and spiritually.

Because of her knowledge, her passion, and her work ethic she has caught the attention of and is now working with and being mentored by top motivational speakers and multi-millionaire entrepreneurs like Jim Britt, best-selling author of over 16 books and Jim Lutes, who is one of the most sought-after personal development experts in the field. She has also caught the attention of and is being endorsed by Robert Wright, Founder of the American Anti-Cancer Institute and author of 'Killing Cancer Not People". In addition to educating groups and corporations about the benefits of a simple health program, she has also been successful in speaking about her experiences with severe anxiety issues, to youth and women's groups about how she has been able to overcome self-hate and food addiction issues, as well as her intense fear of people! Young and mature audiences alike love her funny, yet honest approach to these issues that many women face, and she leaves her audiences laughing and shedding a few tears, but always changed! Comfortable in both the corporate arena as well as in a Christian setting, Tracee has a way of attracting and drawing her audience in. She speaks to corporations and groups about goal setting and life balance in her workshop, "Make Up Your Mind" and how to stay healthy and prevent disease with simple tips in "Get MAD About Cancer".

Tracee credits her success to her faith in God and her "incredible" family who has supported her in every endeavor. Her family has a passion for making a significant difference in the lives of others through mission work, as well as personal and corporate support. They are active supporters and board members of several drug & alcohol recovery programs.

Tracee is a woman of faith, a devoted mother and wife, and she is a loving grandmother. She is a woman of significance and integrity, who speaks from her heart.

To contact Tracee or to find out more about her programs and workshops, go to her website TraceeRandall.com.

Contact Tracee@TraceeRandall.com

Made in the USA
Charleston, SC
30 December 2015